MINUTE
GUIDE TO
ACT!
for Windows

Shelley O'Hara

alpha
books

A Division of Macmillan Computer Publishing
A Prentice Hall Macmillan Company
201 West 103rd Street, Indianapolis, Indiana 46290 USA

©1994 by Alpha Books

International Standard Book Number: 1-56761-539-2

Library of Congress Catalog Card Number: 94-79165

96 95 94   8 7 6 5 4 3 2 1

Interpretation of the printing code: the rightmost number of the first series of numbers is the year of the book's printing; the rightmost number of the second series of numbers is the number of the book's printing. For example, a printing code of 94-1 shows that the first printing of the book occurred in 1994.

Printed in the United States of America

Publisher: Marie Butler-Knight
Product Development Manager: Faithe Wempen
Acquisitions Editor: Barry Pruett
Managing Editor: Elizabeth Keaffaber
Production Editor: Michelle Shaw
Copy Editor: Barry Childs-Helton
Cover Designer: Dan Armstrong
Designer: Barbara Kordesh
Indexer: Brad Herriman
Production: Dan Caparo, Brad Chinn, Kim Cofer, Lisa Daugherty, Cynthia Drouin, Jennifer Eberhardt, Erika Millen, Beth Rago, Bobbi Satterfield, Karen Walsh, Robert Wolf

Special thanks to C. Herbert Feltner for ensuring the technical accuracy of this book.

Contents

Introduction

ACT! for Windows is a great way to get organized. It helps you keep track of people (clients, vendors, friends, associates) and pertinent information about those people (names, addresses, phone numbers, etc.). But if this capability was all ACT! provided, it would be little more than a fancy Rolodex. I'm happy to tell you that ACT! is much more than that.

In addition to enabling you to find up-to-date information about your contacts quickly, ACT! gives you a convenient way to schedule meetings, to-do items, and calls. You can also use ACT! to write letters, send faxes, create form letters, and print reports. With all these tools, you have just about everything you need to take care of business. The only thing missing is an easy-to-follow, step-by-step guide teaching you how to use the program and all its features. That's why you need this book.

Why This Book?

This book provides a concise and practical guide to using ACT! for Windows. Each lesson covers how to use a particular ACT! feature, and is designed so you can read the lesson and get up to speed using that feature in 10 minutes or less. You can start from the beginning and work your way through each lesson, or you can pick up and start at any lesson.

Each lesson teaches you why its particular feature is useful, and then explains (in easy-to-follow steps) how to use that feature. For example, if you want to add a contact, simply read Lesson 3, and follow the steps for adding a contact. If you want to customize the fields in your database, read Lesson 4 and follow those steps. You can find what you want readily and in minimum time.

Special Icons

In addition to the explanatory text and steps, you will find icons that highlight special kinds of information:

Plain English sidebars appear whenever a new term is defined. If you aren't familiar with terms and concepts, watch for these flagged paragraphs.

Panic Button sidebars alert you to common mistakes and tell you how to avoid them. These paragraphs also explain how to undo certain features.

Timesaver Tip sidebars explain shortcuts (for example, key combinations) for performing certain tasks.

Conventions Used in This Book

To help you move quickly through the lessons, you will find these conventions throughout the book:

What you type	Information you must type appears in bold, color type.
Items you select	Items you select or keys you press appear in color type.
On-screen text	Messages that display on your screen appear in a bold type.

Acknowledgments

Thanks to Barry Pruett, Faithe Wempen, Michelle Shaw, Barry Childs-Helton, and Herb Feltner.

Trademarks

All terms mentioned in this book that are known to be trademarks or service marks are listed below. In addition, terms suspected of being trademarks or service marks have been appropriately capitalized. Alpha Books cannot attest to the accuracy of this information. Use of a term in this book should not be regarded as affecting the validity of any trademark or service mark.

ACT! is a trademark of Symantec Corporation.

Lesson

Getting Started

In this lesson, you learn how to start and exit ACT!, take a look at the ACT! window, select a menu command, and get help.

Starting ACT!

If you haven't yet installed ACT! on your computer, see the inside front cover of this book. Once ACT! is installed, follow the steps below to start and use the program.

You must be in Windows in order to start ACT! Some computers are set up to start Windows automatically when you turn on the computer. Other computers start you at the DOS prompt, which looks like this: **C:\>**. At the DOS prompt, you need to type WIN and press Enter to start Windows. You see the Program Manager on-screen.

To start ACT! from the Program Manager, follow these steps:

1. Double-click on the ACT! program group icon. The program group window containing the program icon appears (see Figure 1.1 on the following page).

2. Double-click on the ACT! program icon. The ACT! window appears.

If you are starting the program for the first time, you see a blank work area, with only the File and Help menus visible on the menu bar. Using the File menu, you can open a database or create a new database. (More on these later.)

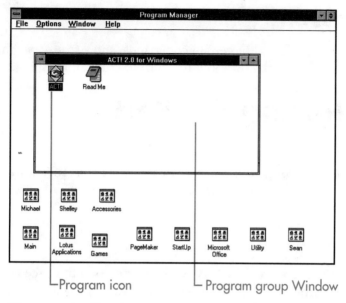

Figure 1.1   The ACT! program group window.

If you have already created a database, that database appears on-screen. If you have several databases, the last one you worked with appears.

Understanding the ACT! Window

ACT! includes several on-screen elements that you will find in most Windows programs. For example, notice the *title bar* and the Maximize, Minimize, and Restore buttons.

Minimize, Maximize, Restore   Click on the *Minimize button* to shrink the window to an icon. Click on the *Maximize button* to expand the window to fill the screen. Click on the *Restore button* to make the window smaller than the entire screen.

In addition to these window controls, the ACT! window includes a *menu bar* for selecting commands, an *icon bar* to use as a shortcut for certain commands, and a *status bar* that includes information about the current contact. Figure 1.2 identifies these elements.

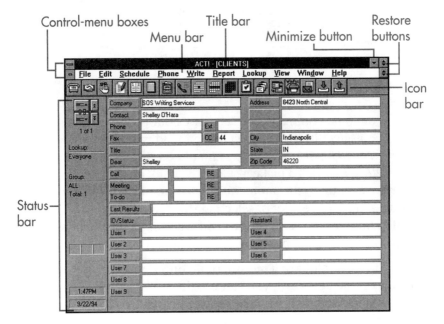

Figure 1.2 The ACT! window.

Selecting Menu Commands

When you want to perform some task in ACT!, such as adding a new contact, you select a menu command. You can find commands in the pull-down menus. To select a command, follow these steps:

1. Click on the menu name in the menu bar. ACT! displays a drop-down list of menu commands (see Figure 1.3 on the following page).

2. Click on the command you want.

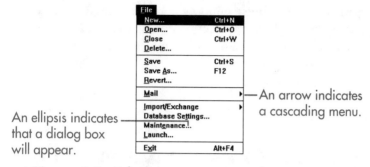

An ellipsis indicates that a dialog box will appear.

An arrow indicates a cascading menu.

Figure 1.3 Selecting a menu command.

For some commands, ACT! carries out the command after you select it. If you select a command with an arrow next to it, ACT! displays a submenu of commands called a *cascading menu*. To make a selection, click on the command you want in the submenu. If the command is followed by an *ellipsis* (three dots), selecting the command displays a dialog box. Make the selections you want in the dialog box, and click on the OK button.

If you don't have a mouse, or if you prefer to keep your hands on the keyboard, you can use the keyboard to select a menu command. Follow these steps:

1. Press the Alt key to activate the menu bar.

2. To open the menu, press the key letter (underlined) in the menu name. For example, to open the File menu, press F.

3. To select a command, press the key letter in the command name.

Try a Shortcut Key! Notice that ACT! displays key combinations next to some commands. You can press the key combination to access the command. For instance, press Ctrl+O to select the File, Open command.

To close a menu without making a selection, press Esc or click outside the menu.

Using the Icon Bar

Under the menu bar, you see a row of *icons* (small buttons with pictures). These icons represent shortcuts to frequently used commands. Instead of selecting a command from a menu, you can click on the icon. For example, click on the Meeting icon to schedule a meeting. Table 1.1 includes a picture of each icon, the icon name, and a short description.

As Is or Your Choice   Table 1.1 lists all the default icons. You can also customize the icon bar.

Table 1.1   The icon bar.

Icon	Icon Name	Description
	Call	Schedules a call
	Meeting	Schedules a meeting
	To-do	Schedules a to-do activity
	Letter	Creates a letter
	Activities	Displays an activity list
	Notes	Displays notes
	History	Displays client history
	Phone List	Displays phone list
	Day View	Displays a day view of scheduled activities
	Week View	Displays a week view of scheduled activities

continues

Table 1.1 Continued

Icon	Icon Name	Description
	Month View	Displays a month view of scheduled activities
	Task List	Displays a task list
	Contact List	Displays a contact list
	Switch Layout	Toggles between current and previous layouts
	Create Message	Displays the Mail menu
	Inbox	Opens your inbox
	Outbox	Opens your outbox

If you have the program WinFAX Pro on your system, you may also have an icon for sending faxes.

Getting Help

To refresh your memory about how to perform a certain task, you can use on-line help. There are two ways to display the Help window, and these ways coincide with how you might look up information in a book. That is, you can look through the table of contents (Help Contents) or you can look through the index (Help Index).

Using the Help Contents

To look through the table of contents, follow these steps:

1. Open the Help menu and select the Contents command. A window displaying different ACT! topics appears (see Figure 1.4 on the following page).

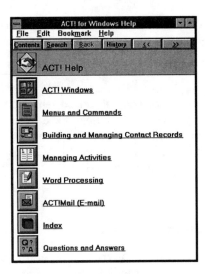

Figure 1.4   Help Contents.

2. Jump to the topic you want by clicking on it. You can jump to any underlined entry.

3. Continue to jump from topic to topic until you find the information you need.

> **Keyboard Shortcut!**   You can also press F1 to display the Help Contents screen.

Using the Help Index

To use the index, follow these steps:

1. Open the Help menu and select the Index command. The Help Index window appears.

2. Click on the letter you want. For example, if the topic you want starts with F, click on F. ACT! displays all Help topics that start with that letter.

3. Click on the underlined topic to jump to that topic. Continue clicking on topics until the information you want is displayed.

> **More Help** You can get context-sensitive help by pressing Shift+F1. The pointer looks like a question mark. Click on the screen item or menu command for which you want help. ACT! displays help for that item or command.

Closing the Help Window

To close the Help window, open its File menu and select the Exit command, or double-click on the Help window's Control-menu box.

Exiting ACT!

When you are finished working in ACT!, you can exit the program. To do so, open the File menu and select the Exit command. You are returned to the Windows Program Manager. You can start another Windows program, or exit Windows and turn off the computer.

> **Shortcut!** To exit ACT! quickly, press Alt+F4 or double-click on the program's Control-menu box.

In this lesson you learned how to start ACT! and became familiar with the program window; Lesson 2 explains how to create a new databases.

Lesson

Creating a New Database

In this lesson, you learn how to create a new database, enter your record information, and take a look through the default fields.

Creating a New Database

ACT! includes a DEMO database you can open and work with when you want to experiment with the program. (Opening a database is covered in Lesson 6.) When you are ready to create your own database, you can create a new one. You can create and save as many database files as you want. For instance, you may want one database for your business clients, one for your personal associates, and one for your vendors.

To create a new database, follow these steps:

1. Open the File menu and select the New command. The New File dialog box appears (see Figure 2.1), which enables you to select the type of file you want to create.

> **Keyboard Shortcut!** Press Ctrl+N to quickly access the New File dialog box.

Figure 2.1 The New File dialog box.

2. Click on Database. The New Database dialog box appears (see Figure 2.2 below). Enter the name you want to use for your database.

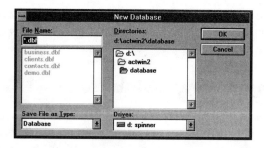

Figure 2.2 The New Database dialog box.

3. Type a name (up to eight characters) for the database. ACT! uses the extension .DBF.

4. Click on the OK button. The Enter "My Record" Information dialog box appears.

Entering Your Record Information

When you are creating a new database, ACT! includes one record with information about you, the user. This record enables you to include your company information in reports and letters. Also, suppose you have a meeting and want to schedule it, but the meeting doesn't pertain to any of your contacts. You can schedule the meeting using your record. (Scheduling meetings is covered in Lesson 11.)

You enter information about your company in the Enter "My Record" Information dialog box (see Figure 2.3). If you completed this information when you installed the program, some or all of the fields may be complete.

```
Enter "My Record" Information
Company:  SOS Writing Services          The "My Record" contains
Name:     Shelley O'Hara                information about the owner
                                        or manager of the database.
Address:  6423 North Central
                                        Use this record to schedule
                                        activities not associated with
                                        other contacts.

                                        [ Use from current database ]
City:     Indianapolis
State:    IN      Zip:  46220           [ Select from import file ]
Country:  United States                 [ Select from current group ]
Phone:            Ext:                  [ OK ]      [ Cancel ]
```

Figure 2.3   The Enter "My Record" Information dialog box.

Follow these steps to complete the record:

1. Press Tab to move to the field in which you want to make an entry, or click in the field.

2. Type or change the existing entry.

3. Follow steps 1 and 2 for each field you want to enter or change. The dialog box includes fields for your company name, your name, address, city, state, ZIP code, country, phone number, and extension.

> **Fields and Records**   A field is one piece of information about a particular person; for instance, a phone number. One set of fields is a record.

4. When you are finished making entries, click on the OK button. You are asked whether the information is correct.

5. Click on the Yes button if the information is correct. If the information isn't correct, click on No, make any changes, click on OK, and then choose Yes. You are prompted for a password.

6. If you want to assign a password to the database, type it and click on the OK button. Otherwise, just click on the OK button.

Your record is now complete. ACT! creates the appropriate database files, and displays the contact database screen. Here you can enter information about your contacts.

Understanding the Default Fields

ACT! uses two screens of information for each contact you enter. The first screen is displayed by default, and includes the most commonly used fields. The second screen includes fields for additional information, such as alternative contact names, e-mail information, and more.

The First Screen

The first screen includes common information such as the company name, contact name, address, city, state, ZIP codes, FAX number, assistant, and more (see Figure 2.4). In addition to these fields, ACT! includes user fields that you can customize to fit your needs. Table 2.1 explains some of the fields you might not understand at first.

Think About What You Need!   Keep in mind that once a database is set up, it is difficult to make changes to the structure of the database. Spend some time thinking about the information you need to do business, and then customize the database accordingly.

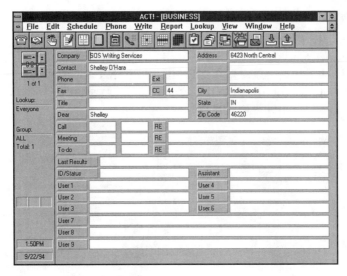

Figure 2.4 The first contact screen.

Table 2.1 ACT! default fields on screen 1.

Field Name	Description
Ext	Contact's extension number.
CC	Contact's country code.
Dear	Salutation or greeting you want to use when addressing this person in letters.
Call, Meeting, To-do	Displays calls, meetings, and to-do activities scheduled for this contact.
Last Results	Results from your last contact (for example, "pending sale").
ID/Status	Customer ID number or status information.
Assistant	Contact's assistant.
User 1-9	You can customize these fields so they fit your business needs. Customizing the contact screen is covered in Lesson 4.

Second Screen

To move to the second screen, click on the Switch Layout
icon or open the View menu, select the Layout command,
and select Contact 2 from the submenu that appears. Figure
2.5 displays the fields in the second contact screen. Table 2.2
explains the fields in this contact screen.

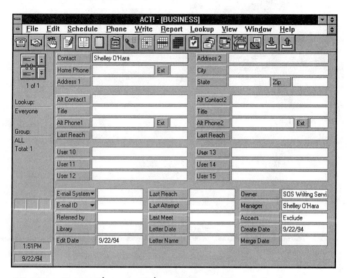

Figure 2.5   The second contact screen.

Table 2.2   ACT! default fields on screen 2.

Field(s)	Description
Contact	The name from screen 1.
Home Phone, Ext, Address 1, Address 2	The home phone number and address information for the contact.
Alt Contact 1, Title, Alt Phone 1, Ext, Last Reach	An alternative contact—for example, the contact's assistant or supervisor. Enter the title, phone number, extension, and date this contact was last reached in these fields.

Field(s)	Description
Alt Contact 2, Title, Alt Phone 2, Ext, Last Reach User 10-15	An additional alternative contact. You can customize these fields so that they fit your business needs.
E-mail System, E-mail ID E-mail information about the contact. Referred by	Enter e-mail information. Name of person who referred this contact or referral source (trade show, advertisement, etc.)
Library	Name of the library file attached to this contact.
Edit Date, Last Reach, Last Attempt, Last Meet, Letter Date, Letter Name	ACT! automatically records the last time the contact record was edited, the last time you were in contact with this person, the last time you attempted to contact this person, the last meeting date, the date of the last letter you sent, and the letter name.
Owner	Your company name.
Manager	Your name.
Access	Access level (used for networked versions).
Create Date	Date you created the record.
Merge Date	Date you merged the record.

Back to Screen 1 To return to the first screen, press F6; click on the Previous Layout icon; or open the View menu, select Layout, and select Contact 1.

Saving the Database

Each time you add a new record (covered in Lesson 3), you click on the Save button to save the record and the database. Each time you schedule a call or meeting or make a change, the database is saved also. Therefore, you don't have to worry too much about saving the database.

New Name   If you want to save a database under a new name, open the File menu and select the Save As command. Type a new name and click on the OK button.

In this lesson you learned how to create a database; Lesson 3 teaches you how to add contacts.

Lesson

Adding Contacts

In this lesson, you learn how to add a new contact, enter data into the contact screen, and attach notes to a contact.

Adding a New Contact

The purpose of using ACT! is to enter and keep track of the many contacts you have. You may want to keep track of clients, personal associates, business associates, vendors, employees—whomever. To enter a new contact, follow these steps:

1. Open the Edit menu and select the New Contact command. The Insert Contact dialog box appears (see Figure 3.1 on the following page).

> **Keyboard Shortcut!** Press Ins to quickly access the Insert Contact dialog box.

2. Do one of the following:

To create the new contact and use all the default values you have assigned, select Default. You can create default values that are used in certain fields. This feature is covered in Lesson 5.

Figure 3.1 The Insert Contact dialog box.

To create the new contact and use all the values from the primary fields, select Primary. ACT! will use the same values for the primary fields in the current record, including the company, address, city, state, ZIP code, phone number, and country code. You can set which fields are primary fields. See Lesson 5 for more information.

To create the new contact and use all the values from the current record, select All.

Several Similar Contacts?   Use the Primary option if you have to enter several contacts from the same company.

ACT! displays a new record on-screen. Some of the fields may be completed. For example, if you selected All, the record includes values from the current record.

Entering Contact Information

To get the most from ACT!, you'll need to take some time to collect and enter all the information you have about a contact. Your investment of time will pay off when you can quickly find the information you need. As mentioned, you have two screens of contact information to complete for each contact. This section explains how to enter information.

Entering Data Into a Field

To enter data into a field, follow these steps:

1. Move to the field you want, either by clicking in it or pressing Tab.

2. Type the entry and press Tab. ACT! moves to the next field, using this order: Company, Contact, Phone, Ext, Fax, CC (Country Code), Title, Dear, Address, City, State, ZIP Code.

> **Make a Mistake?** If you make a mistake, press Shift+Tab to move backward through the fields to find it, or simply click in the field you want to change. Make the change and continue entering information.

3. Follow steps 1 and 2 for each field in the first screen. When you complete all the fields in the first record, you can move to and complete the second screen.

4. To move to the second screen, click on the Switch Layout icon—or open the View menu, select the Layout command, and select Contact 2 from the submenu.

5. Complete all the fields for the second contact screen.

6. When you have completed all the fields in the record, click on the Save button to save the database and the new record.

> **Cancel the Entry** If you enter a contact by mistake, you can click on the Cancel button or press Esc. ACT! prompts you to confirm the cancellation. Click on the Yes button.

Using the Popup Menus

To make it easy to enter common values, ACT! gives you *popup menus* for some fields. For example, you can display a popup list of common titles (CEO, Chairman, Director, etc.). Rather than type the entry, you can select the entry from the list.

To use a popup menu, follow these steps:

1. Move to the field for which you want to display the popup.

2. Press F2 to display the popup (see Figure 3.2 below).

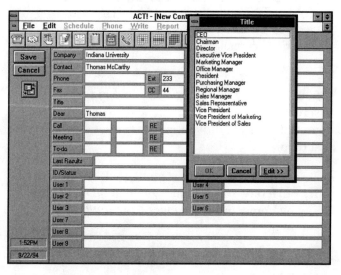

Figure 3.2   A popup menu.

Nothing Happens   If you press F2 and nothing appears, it means this field does not have a popup menu assigned. To change which fields have popups, see Lesson 4.

3. Click on the item you want.

4. Click on the OK button.

Customize the Popups   You can edit the
popup menus so they contain entries applicable
to your business. See Lesson 5.

Table 3.1 lists the fields for which popups are available
as well as describes what the popups include.

Table 3.1   Fields with supplemental popups.

Field	Description
Screen 1	
Phone	Displays common cities and area codes.
Fax	Displays common area codes.
Title	Displays common job titles.
CC	Displays country codes.
City	Displays common cities and area codes.
State	Displays states and state abbreviations.
Zip Code	Initially is blank, but can be used to list common ZIP codes.
Call, Meeting, To-do	Displays a calendar for scheduling a call, meeting, or to-do. The popup for the next field in this section displays a day-timer so you can select a time. The RE popup contains a list of call, meeting, and to-do descriptions (*Confirm appointment*, *Follow up*, for example).

continues

Table 3.1 Continued

Field	Description
Last Results	Lists common phrases for last results (*Got appointment, Requested more information*, etc.)
ID/Status	Lists types of contacts—*Competitor, Customer, Friend, Prospect*, etc.
Screen 2	
Home Phone, Alt Phone 1, Alt Phone 2	Displays common area codes.
City	Displays common cities.
State	Displays states and state abbreviations.
Title	Lists common titles.
Referred by	Lists common sources of referrals (Trade show, for example).
Access	Includes two options: Exclude and Include.

Fields ACT! Will Enter for You

As you work your way through each contact screen, you can skip the fields you don't need. You can also skip fields that ACT! enters for you automatically. For example, after you enter the contacts, you can use ACT! to schedule meetings, calls, and to-do activities. When you use ACT! for scheduling, ACT! automatically makes a note on the contact screen that describes the call, meeting, or to-do item. ACT! also updates the fields such as Last Reach, Last Attempt, and so on if you use ACT! to track your activities. Lessons 10, 11, and 12 cover scheduling and managing your schedule.

Attaching Notes

You want ACT! to keep track of who you talked to, when, and what was said. The contact screens include fields for tracking when a call was made, and you can use the Last Results field to track what happened. In addition to this field, you may want to keep more detailed notes about a contact (or a scheduled activity, such as a call). To do so, you can attach a note.

Follow these steps to add a note:

1. Open the View menu and select the Notes command. ACT! opens a note window (see Figure 3.3).

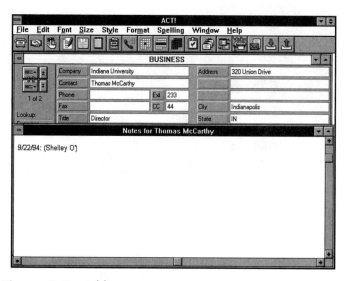

Figure 3.3   Adding a note.

Shortcut!   Press F9 or click on the Notes button to quickly open a note window.

2. Type the text for the note. You can type as much text as needed.

3. To close the note window, double-click on the Control-menu box.

You are returned to the contact screen. ACT! displays the **Note** indicator in the status bar to remind you that a note has been attached (see Figure 3.4 below).

To edit or view the note, open the View menu and select the Notes command; press F9 or click on the Notes button. You may want, for example, to review any notes you made for a contact before you call or have a meeting with that contact.

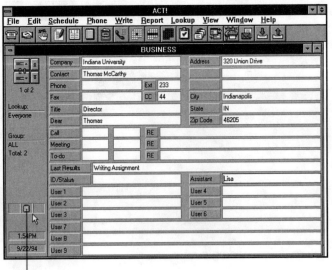

Note indicator

Figure 3.4 A contact with a note attached.

In this lesson you learned how to add a contact; in Lesson 4 you learn how to customize the contact screen.

Lesson

Customizing the Contact Screens

In this lesson, you learn how to customize the contact screens by using a description file and by modifying field attributes. You also learn how to use the reference library.

Using a Description File

The makers of ACT! anticipated that various specific groups of people would use ACT!, for example, small business owners, real estate agents, salespeople, and others. Each group needs to keep track of different types of information. To meet this need, ACT! created customized contact screens with customized fields.

> **Description File**   A file of user-defined settings, such as field labels, field attributes, and field data types. The description file is saved with the database.

Before you customize the default screens, you may want to see whether one of the predefined customized screens (called description files) are applicable to your needs. ACT! includes 8 description files you can use, as described in the following list:

BUSINESS includes fields for Annual Billing, Client Class, Service Frequency, Service Rate, Contact Class, Partner Assigned, Now Retain, Reason Retain, and Special Needs.

DEFAULT is the default database.

DEMO is the database file used for the DEMO database.

INSURANC includes fields for Age, Dependents, Birthdate, Customer Since, Reason, Interest Area, Coverage Now, Proposed Type, Dollar Value.

MANAGER is especially useful for sales managers. Includes fields for Next Objective, Last Order $, YTD Revenue, Business Class, Contact Class, Credit Status, Hotbuttons, Memberships, and Reminder.

PROJLDR is an abbreviation for Project Leader. It includes fields for Start Date, Due Date, Probable Date, Dept. Assigned, Group Leader, and Expertise.

RESRE means Residential Real Estate. Includes fields for Price, Bed/Bath/Garage, Living, Dining, Map Coord, Legal Description, Amenities, Bonus, Expertise, Commission Rate, Lot, Reduction, Contract, Expire, and Close Date.

SALES includes fields for Forecast, Probability, Competition, YTD Revenue, Last Order, etc.

To use one of these description files, follow these steps:

1. Open the File menu and select the Database Settings command. The Database Settings dialog box appears (see Figure 4.1 below).

Figure 4.1   Database Settings dialog box.

2. Click on the Apply button. The Apply Description File dialog box appears, listing the available description files (see Figure 4.2 below).

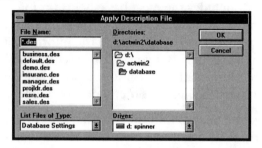

Figure 4.2   Select the description file that you want to attach.

3. In the File Name list, click on the description file you want to use.

4. Click on the OK button. ACT! updates the current database, and displays the user-defined fields for the description file.

> **Return to the Defaults**   You can attach a description file to see the different fields. When you want to return to the default, select the DEFAULT file.

> **Save a Description File**   If you customize a database, you can save the customized fields in a description file that you can attach to other databases. Open the File menu, select the Database Settings command, click on the Save As button, and then type a file name and click on the OK button.

Defining Field Attributes

You will get the most benefit from ACT! if you customize the contact screens so they include information useful to you. By default, ACT! includes the most basic fields for information (phone number, address, and so on). These fields are recognized as important, and are similar to the information you may keep in a Rolodex. But you can also set up and keep track of other information—year-to-date sales amount, commission percentage, last order date, and more.

Take some time to think about what information is useful to you in your business. What information helps you make a sale? What information keeps you up-to-date with your clients? What information helps you make a better presentation?

Once you decide on the information you need to keep, you can customize ACT!'s user fields for your own needs, as described in this section.

Understanding What You Can Change

You can change the field attributes for any of the user fields—and most of the other fields—in the contact screens. When you define the field attributes for a particular field, you can do the following:

- Change the name or field label that is used. For example, you can change **User 1** to **Last Sale Date**.

- Select the type of data that the field should contain. Selecting the data type makes entering data easier. For example, if the field contains a phone number, you can select this as the data type, and ACT! will enter the phone number automatically, in the format (317) 555-9900. You don't have to type the parentheses or the dash.

- Set the field attributes—for example, which fields have popups, and which fields are primary fields?

Changing Field Attributes

Follow these steps to set field attributes:

1. Open the Edit menu and select the Field Attributes command. ACT! displays the Field Attributes dialog box (see Figure 4.3 below).

> **Shortcut!** To display the Field Attributes dialog box quickly, double-click on the field using the *right* mouse button.

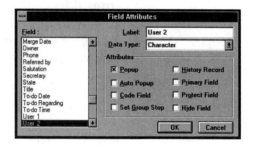

Figure 4.3 The Field Attributes dialog box.

2. In the Field list, click on the field you want to modify. You can change existing fields such as Company or user fields (User 1, User 2, etc.). When you select a field, ACT! displays the label, data type, and attributes for the selected field.

3. To change the name of the field, click in the Label text box, drag across the current entry to select the text, and then type the new label.

4. To change the type of data you enter in a field, display the Data Type drop-down list and select a data type from the list on the following page.

Data Type	Description
Character	You can enter both letters and numbers in the field.
Uppercase	ACT! converts all alphanumeric characters to uppercase.
Date	Type the date in the format **mmddyy**. ACT! formats it as **mm/dd/yy**. ACT! inserts the slashes automatically. You cannot enter letters in the field.
Phone number	You type the nine-digit phone number, and ACT! formats it as **(xxx) xxx-xxxx**. You don't need to type the parentheses or dash.
Numeric	Accepts only numbers, commas, and periods in the field.
Currency	Accepts only numbers, commas, periods, dollar signs, and dashes. Type **9450**, and ACT! formats it as $9,450.
0-9 only	Accepts only the numbers 0-9 in the field; you cannot type letters or any other characters.

Data Type	Description
Time	Accepts only times in the format **hh:mm**. You can also type **A** or **P** for a.m. or p.m.

Can't Make Changes? If the arrow is dimmed next to the Data Type list, it means you cannot change the data type for this field. You cannot modify the field type for some of ACT!'s default fields, such as Call Date.

5. To activate the field attribute options, click in the check box. When an option is checked, it is activated. You can set any of the following:

Check...	To Do This...
Popup	Make a popup menu available.
Auto Popup	Display the popup automatically when you move to this field. Note that this option is available only when the Popup check box is checked.
Code Field	Use two columns in the popup (the description and a code). This option is available only when the Popup check box is selected.

continues

Check...	*To Do This...*
Set Group Stop	Assign a group stop to this field. When you press Tab+Enter, **ACT!** moves to the next field with this attribute.
History Record	Track any changes, deletions, or additions to this field in the client history.
Primary Field	Make this a primary field. When you create a new record, you can copy the primary fields from the current record to the new record (see Lesson 3).
Protect Field	Protect this field from being modified.
Hide Field	Hide the field; the field will not appear in the contact screen.

6. Click on the OK button when you are finished completing field attributes. **ACT!** closes the dialog box and updates the field.

Using the Reference Library

Another way you can make the contact screens more pertinent is to attach and use a *reference library*. A reference library is basically a word processing document that can be displayed on-screen. For example, suppose that you use a sales script when calling customers. You could type and attach the script to customer contacts. You might also keep a price list or a discount list in the reference library.

You can have as many reference libraries as you want, but only one can be attached to a contact at one time.

To create and attach the reference library, follow these steps:

1. Type the information using the word processing program. (See Lesson 15 for information on creating a document.)

2. Save the document as described in Lesson 18. Be sure to save the file with the extension .WPD, and in the directory C:\ACTWIN2\DOCS.

3. Display the second contact screen for the contact. This contact should be the one to which you want to attach the file.

4. In the Library field, type the file name you used when you created the file. Be sure to type the entire file name, including extension.

When you want to display, open the View menu and select the Reference Library command, or press Shift+F3. You see the document you created on-screen (see Figure 4.4 on the following page). When you are finished with the document, double-click on the Control-menu box.

Reference document

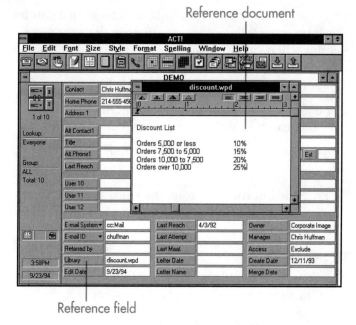

Reference field

Figure 4.4 A reference file attached.

In this lesson you learned to customize the contact screen; Lesson 5 explains some of the data-entry shortcuts.

Lesson

Data-Entry Shortcuts

In this lesson, you learn some ways you can speed up entering contacts, including how to set up and use default values and how to modify the popup menus.

Defining Default Values

Remember that when you add a new contact, you can elect to use the default values, the primary values, or all values. You can set up and use default values if you use the same field information in many of your records. For instance, if most of your clients are based in Florida, you may want to enter FL as the state. If most of your clients are within the same area code, you can enter the default area code. You can set up a default value for any field in the contact screen. This section explains how to create and use default values.

Creating Default Values

The first step is to create the default values. To do so, follow these steps:

1. Open the Edit menu and select the Field Defaults command. ACT! displays a blank record named Field Defaults (see Figure 5.1 on the following page).

2. Click in the field for which you want to enter a default value, or press Tab to move to the field.

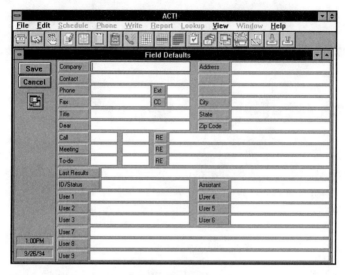

Figure 5.1   Entering field defaults.

3. Type the default value you want to use. ACT! will use what you enter for all records you create using the default values. For example, if you type **317** in the first part of the phone field and insert a new record using the default values, ACT! will display the new record with **317** in the phone field.

Follow steps 2 and 3 for each field for which you want to set a default value. You can enter default values for any fields on the first or second contact screens.

4. When you have completed entering the default values, click on the Save button. ACT! returns you to the contact screen.

Using Default Values

When you want to use the default values in a record, follow these steps:

1. Open the Edit menu and select the New Contact command. The Insert Contact dialog box appears.

2. Click on the Default button. ACT! creates a record and fills in the default values you defined.

Entering Several Similar Records

When you have several contacts with similar information, you can speed up entering the information by using the same information in several records. For example, suppose that you are entering several contacts with the same company name, address, state, city, ZIP, and phone number. Rather than enter this information over and over for each contact, you can enter the information for the first contact and use the same information for the remaining contacts.

To enter similar records, you can use one of two methods:

- You can insert a new contact and select All. ACT! will use the same values for all the fields. You can then modify any fields that are different.

- You can insert a new contact and select Primary. ACT! will use the same values for all primary fields. By default, the primary fields are address, city, company, fax, phone, state, and ZIP code. You can also change which fields are primary (and which aren't) by modifying the field attributes, as described in Lesson 4.

Editing the Popup Menus

When you are entering data in some fields, you can access a popup list of common values. For instance, for the State field, you can press F2 to display a popup list of all states. You can select the state from the list rather than type it. If the popup list doesn't include the values you need, you can add to them. You can also modify items and delete items you don't use, as described in this section.

Note: You can also change which fields have popups by modifying the field attributes. This feature is covered in Lesson 4.

Adding Entries

To add an entry to a popup list, follow these steps:

1. Move to the field that contains the popup and press F2. ACT! displays the popup list.

2. Click on the Edit button. ACT! displays additional buttons in the dialog box.

3. Click on the Add button. You see the Add String dialog box. Here you type the entry you want to add (see Figure 5.2 below).

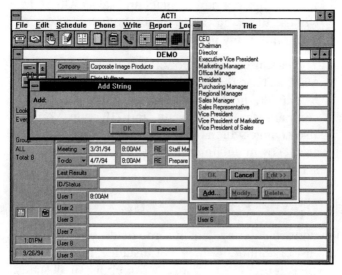

Figure 5.2 Adding a new popup entry to the title popup.

4. Type the new entry.

5. Click on the OK button. ACT! adds the entry to the popup list. The list remains open on-screen.

6. Click on the OK button to close the popup list.

Modifying Entries

If the popup entry contains an incorrect or incomplete entry, you can modify the entry so that it is correct. Follow these steps:

1. Move to the field that has the popup you want to edit.

2. Press F2 to display the popup list.

> **Nothing Happens**   If you press F2 and nothing appears, it means the field does not have a popup. If you are in the incorrect field, move to the correct field and press F2. Or if you want to create a popup list for the fields, modify the field attributes, as described in Lesson 4.

3. Click on the Edit button. ACT! displays additional buttons in the popup list.

4. Click on the entry you want to change.

5. Click on the Modify button. You see the Modify String dialog box (see Figure 5.3 on the following page).

6. Make the changes you want.

7. Click on the OK button. ACT! returns you to the popup list.

8. To close the popup list, click on the OK button.

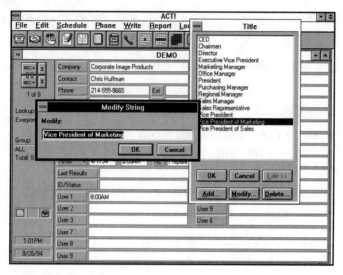

Figure 5.3   Editing a popup entry.

Deleting an Entry

The purpose of the popup list is to make entering common values as quick as possible. This purpose is defeated if extraneous entries make the popup list too long and un-wieldy. In this case, you may want to get rid of the values you don't need. To do so, follow these steps:

1. Move to the field that has the popup you want to edit.

2. Press F2 to display the popup list.

3. Click on the Edit button. ACT! displays additional buttons in the popup list.

4. Click on the entry you want to delete.

5. Click on the Delete button. ACT! prompts you to confirm the deletion (see Figure 5.4 on the following page).

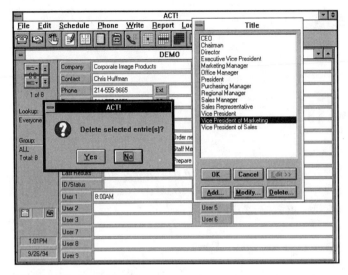

Figure 5.4   Deleting a popup entry.

6. Click on the Yes button to delete the entry. To cancel the deletion, click on the No button.

7. Click on the OK button to close the popup list.

8. When you are finished editing the popup list, choose OK.

> **Delete Several Entries**   To delete several entries, display the popup list and click on the Edit button. Click on the first entry you want to delete. Hold down the Ctrl key and click on the next entry you want to delete. Ctrl+click on all the entries, and then click on the Delete button.

In this lesson you learned about different data entry shortcuts; in Lesson 6 you learn how to edit contact information.

Lesson

Editing Contacts

In this lesson, you learn how to open a database, select a record, edit a contact or group of contacts, and delete a contact or group of contacts.

Opening a Database

If you have only one database, you don't have to worry about opening it, because when you start the program, ACT! opens the last database that was used. There may be times, however, when you do need to open a database. For example, if you close your database, you will need to reopen it to work on the contacts. Or if you have more than one database, you can open the one you need.

To open a database, follow these steps:

1. Open the File menu and select the Open command. ACT! displays the Open File dialog box (see Figure 6.1 below), listing all the database files (DBF) in the current directory.

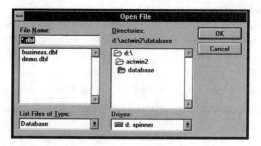

Figure 6.1 The Open File dialog box.

Keyboard Shortcut! Press Ctrl+O to display the Open File dialog box.

2. In the File Name list, click on the database you want to open.

3. Click on OK. ACT! displays the database on-screen.

My Database Isn't Listed! By default, ACT! stores all database files in the directory \ACTWIN2\DATABASE. If your database is in another drive or directory, you have to change to that directory or drive. To change directories, double-click on the directory name in the Directories list. To change drives, display the Drives drop-down list and select the drive.

Moving from Record to Record

When you start ACT! or open a database, ACT! displays the first record in that database. (The records are sorted by company name; therefore the first record would be the first company name in alphabetical order.) When you want to edit information, you first have to find and display the record you want. This section explains how to move among the records using the status bar and keyboard. This method works fine when you have only a few records to look through.

When your database contains many records, however, you may want to use a quicker method—for example, looking up a particular record. Lookups are covered in the next lesson.

The status bar along the left side of the contact screen gives information about the current record, and provides buttons that enable you to move from record to record (see

Figure 6.2). Table 6.1 explains how to move from record to record using these status bar buttons or the keyboard.

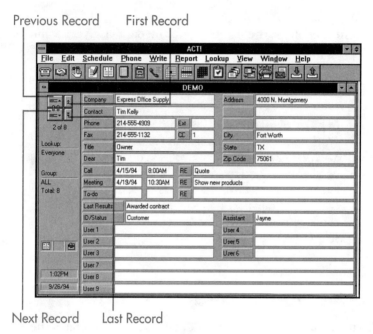

Figure 6.2 Status bar buttons.

Table 6.1 Moving from record to record.

To move to	Click on this button	Or press
Next record		PgDn
Previous record		PgUp
First record		
Last Record		

The status bar reminds you of which record you are viewing; it also shows the total number of records. For example, if you see **8 of 10**, you know you are viewing the eighth record in a group of ten.

Editing Contact Information

The contact information in your database is only as reliable as the information you enter. If someone moves or changes jobs, or a phone number changes, you should update the contact record accordingly. You can edit a single contact record or a group of records, as described here.

Editing a Single Record

To edit a record, follow these steps:

1. Display the record you want to change.

> **Finding the Record**   You can use the Next Record, Previous Record, First Record, and Last Record buttons to scroll through the records until you find the one you want. Or you can search for a particular record. See Lesson 7 for looking up a record.

2. Click in the field you want to change.

3. Add, modify, or delete the entry as needed.

To add text, click where you want the new text to be; then start typing. To delete text, drag across the entry to select it. Press Del or Backspace to delete the selection. Or type the new entry; ACT! will replace the selection with the new entry.

You can also copy or cut an entry, and then paste it to another field. To do so, drag across the entry to select it, open the Edit menu and select either Cut or Copy. Click in the field into which you want to paste the selection. Open the Edit menu and select the Paste command. ACT! pastes the entry.

Editing a Group of Records

In your contact database, you may have several contacts from the same company. If some bit of information for that company changes—for instance, the phone number—you'll need to update all the records accordingly. Rather than do so one after another after another, you can edit the group all at once.

To edit a group of records, follow these steps:

1. Create a lookup group that contains the records you want to edit. (Lesson 7 explains how to create a lookup group.)

> **Lookup Group**   A lookup group is a set of contacts—for instance, all contacts from a particular company or in a particular state.

2. Open the Edit menu and select the Current Lookup command. ACT! displays a blank record on-screen called Edit Lookup (see Figure 6.3 on the following page).

3. Click in the field or press Tab until you move to the field you want to change.

4. Type the new entry. The entry you type in this field will be used in all records in the lookup group.

5. Follow steps 3 and 4 for each field you want to change. You can change any fields in either of the contact screens.

6. Click on the OK button. ACT! reminds you that the change will affect all records in the lookup group.

7. Click on the Yes button to make the changes. To cancel the changes, click on the No button. If you confirmed the change, ACT! updates all records in the lookup group.

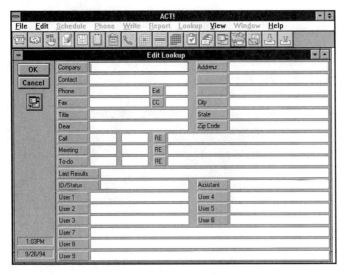

Figure 6.3   Editing a group of records.

Deleting Contacts

Another good habit of contact management is to delete contacts you no longer need. If your database contains extraneous information, it will be harder to find records you need. You can delete a single contact or a group of contacts.

> **Caution**   Be sure that you no longer need any of the information. All the contact information (name, address, phone number, history, and notes) will be deleted. You cannot undo a contact deletion.

Deleting a Single Contact

To delete a contact, follow these steps:

1. Display the contact you want to delete.

2. Open the Edit menu and select the Delete Contact command. ACT! warns you that the deletion cannot be undone; then it asks you to select what to delete—the contact, or all contacts in the lookup group (see Figure 6.4).

Figure 6.4   Deleting a contact.

Keyboard Shortcut   Press Ctrl+Del to quickly delete a contact.

3. Click on the Contact button. You are prompted to confirm the deletion.

4. Click on the Yes button. ACT! deletes the contact and all associated data. To cancel the deletion, click on the No button.

Deleting a Group of Contacts

In some cases, you may want to delete several contacts. For instance, suppose your sales territory includes six states. Your sales manager decides the territory is too large for one person and assigns someone else the contacts in one of your

states. You can turn over all the contact information to your
sales associate; then delete the contacts in that state from
your database.

Save Contacts   You can save contacts from
a lookup to a new database, as described in
Lesson 23.

To delete a group of contacts, follow these steps:

1. Create a lookup group that contains the records you
want to edit. (Lesson 7 explains how to create a
lookup group.)

2. Open the Edit menu and select the Delete Contact
command. ACT! displays a warning and asks you
whether you want to delete the contact or the
lookup.

3. Click on the Lookup button. You are prompted to
confirm the deletion.

4. Click on the Yes button. ACT! deletes all contacts—
and all associated contact data—for the lookup
group. To cancel the deletion, click on the No
button.

In this lesson you learned how to edit contact information and delete contacts; in Lesson 7 you learn how to look
up a particular contact or group of contacts.

Lesson

Looking Up Contacts

7

In this lesson, you learn how to look up a particular contact or a group of contacts, using several different methods.

What Is a Lookup?

A *lookup* has two purposes. First, you can use it to find a particular contact—for instance, you can look up a contact with the last name Riley. Second, you can use it to group contacts—for instance, you can look up all contacts in South Carolina.

ACT! provides several ways to perform a lookup.

- **Predefined lookups** Using the commands in the Lookup menu, you can look up a contact by company, first name, last name, phone, city, state, ZIP, or ID/Status.

- **Keyword** You can search for a particular word contained in a field. For example, you know that you and a contact discussed a project called ON-TIME, and that you made a note of it in the contact screen, but you can't remember the contact. You can search all fields for the words ON-TIME.

- **Custom lookups** With a custom lookup, you specify exactly what you are looking for. For instance, you could find all contacts who have had a call date within the past three days *and* have a certain status.

The rest of this lesson explains the different lookup methods.

Automatic Lookups   When you use the scheduling features, you can have ACT! create a lookup group of all contacts with scheduled activities. You can then move quickly through the contacts and update the results of the calls, meetings, and to-do items. Scheduling is covered in Lessons 10–12.

Once the lookup is created, you can work with this subset of records. You can scroll through them without looking through the entire group of records. You can also delete a lookup group or edit all records in a lookup group, as described in Lesson 6.

Simple Lookups

In many cases, you want to look up a contact based on a common field entry, such as the last name. ACT! anticipates this need and includes commands for common lookup fields in the Lookup menu. You can use simple lookups to find or group a contact quickly. For instance, suppose you want to display the contact record for a client named Frankie Brown. You can search for the contact by using a first-name lookup. Or suppose you want to do a target mailing to all your contacts in a certain neighborhood. You could do a lookup based on ZIP code.

This section explains how to perform a simple lookup, and how to return to all contacts.

Looking Up a Contact Using Common Fields

To look up a contact by company, first or last name, phone number, city, state, ZIP, or ID/Status, follow these steps:

1. Open the Lookup menu.

2. Select the field you want to look up and group by.
You can choose from the following fields: Company, First Name, Last Name, Phone, City, State, Zip
Code, or ID/Status. ACT! displays a dialog box that
prompts you to type the entry you want to match
(see Figure 7.1 below).

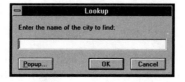

Figure 7.1   Looking up an entry based on the city field.

3. Type the entry you want to match. For instance, to
find and group all contacts in Atlanta, choose City
from the Lookup menu and then type **Atlanta**.

Use The Popup Menu   If the field has a
popup menu, you can choose the Popup button in
the dialog box to display a list of choices. Click
on the option you want; then click on the OK
button.

4. Click on the OK button. ACT! groups and displays
all matching contacts.

If you did a first-name search, you may have only one
contact displayed. If you wanted to group contacts—for
instance, if you looked up the contacts on the basis of
state—you may have several contacts displayed. ACT! lists
the contacts alphabetically. The status bar reflects the current lookup and the number of records in the lookup group
(see Figure 7.2 on the following page).

ACT! sorts lookups on the basis of the field you used as the lookup. For example, if you looked up the contacts by company, the records are sorted by company. If you looked up contacts by last name, the records are sorted by last name. For more information on sorting, see Lesson 9.

Lookup indicator

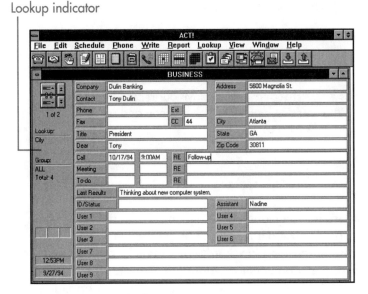

Figure 7.2 A lookup group.

No Contacts Match If you get the message that no matching contacts are found, click on the OK button and try again. Be sure you are searching on the right field, and that you typed the matching entry correctly. If you try again and still get no matches, you may want to try a different type of lookup, as described later in this lesson.

Returning to All Contacts

A lookup group is handy when you want to work with just a subset of your contacts. When you want to return to the entire group of contacts, you can do so by following these steps:

1. Open the Lookup menu.

2. Select the Everyone command. ACT! displays all records in the database.

> **Your Record**   To display your record information quickly, open the Lookup menu and select the My Record command.

Keyword Lookups

If you are having trouble finding a match using the company name, first or last name, ZIP code, phone, city, state, or ID, you can search for a keyword. For instance, you can look up and group all contacts for whom you use the word *promotion*. ACT! will search all field and all contact information for this word and then group the matching records.

To look up and group contacts based on a word used anywhere in the contact record, follow these steps:

1. Open the Lookup menu and select the Keyword command. ACT! displays the Keyword Search dialog box (see Figure 7.3 on the following page). In this dialog box, you can type the word or phrase you want to find.

2. Type the word or phrase you want to find. Keyword searches aren't case sensitive; therefore, you can type the entry using any combination of case (*PROMO, promo, Promo*). ACT! finds matching entries, regardless of case.

Figure 7.3   Type the word or phrase you want to find.

Use a Wildcard   In the keyword search, you can use a wildcard (*) to stand for and match any characters in that position. For example, type **pr*** to find all words that start with *pr*. Type ***tion** to find all words that end in *tion*.

3. Click on the OK button. ACT! searches the database and groups and displays all records that contain the keyword.

Query Lookups

If you have tried a simple lookup and a keyword search and aren't getting the results you want, you can use another method—a *query lookup*. You can look up contacts on the basis of other fields in the contact screen.

Query   A query is a more complex search method. ACT! compares the entries in the query screen to records in the database and displays matching entries.

To create a simple query, follow these steps:

1. Open the Lookup menu and select the Other command. ACT! displays a blank screen. If this is the first time you have created a query, the screen is titled Query.

Query: What Query Is That?   If you have
created and saved another query, the last query
screen is displayed. This query is named by
default lastqry.qry (see Figure 7.4 below). The
query screen is similar to the Edit Lookup and Field
Default screens. You enter the matching values in the
appropriate fields.

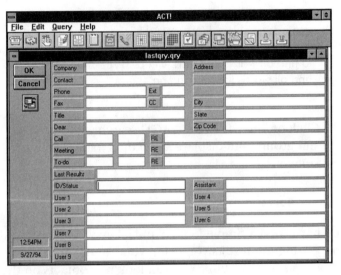

Figure 7.4   Creating a query.

2. Click in (or press Tab to move to) the field on
which you want to search.

3. Type the entry you want to match. If the field
contains a popup, you can press F2 and enter the
value using the popup menu.

Follow steps 2 and 3 for each field you want to
match. For example, suppose that you are planning
a sales trip to Florida and want to find all Last
Results that were "Pending Sale" for follow-up. You
would enter **FL** as the State, and **Pending Sale** in
the Last Results field.

4. When you have entered the values in the fields you want to match, click on the OK button. If you are working with all records, ACT! finds and groups the matching records.

If you are working with a lookup, you are prompted to select whether to include contact records in the current lookup or the current group. (Groups are covered in Lesson 8.) Select Active Group or Active Lookup; then click on the OK button. ACT! finds and groups the matching records.

When you click on the Save button, ACT! saves the query with the name Lastqry.qry. You can use the query again by selecting the Lookup Other command. ACT! displays the same query screen. To execute the query, select Save again.

You can do more with the query features of ACT!, including converting the simple query to a SmartQuery that uses a more complex search strategy. For example, you can use Boolean-logic operators in a SmartQuery to find all call dates after November 8, 1994, or all states that are either Indiana or Illinois. You can save a query with a different name, and add a query to the Lookup menu. For complete information on complex queries, see your ACT! manual.

SmartQuery A complex query that enables you to search on the basis of more than one field for more than one criterion.

Boolean Operations such as AND and OR that you can use to define or broaden a query.

In this lesson you learned how to look up contacts; in Lesson 8 you learn how to create groups of contacts.

Lesson

8

Grouping Contacts

In this lesson, you learn how to work with groups of contacts—how to create, view, modify, and delete a group.

Groups Versus Lookups

In Lesson 7, you learned how to create a lookup group—a set of contacts grouped by a common piece of information such as the company name or state.

In this lesson, you learn how to create a group in which you can individually select which contacts are members of the group. This type of group does not have to share a common piece of information (although they can). You can create a group based on a lookup or based on all contacts.

Even though the contacts are grouped into subsets, you don't have to worry about duplicate records or about updating more than one record. The record is still part of the main database, and can belong to more than one group. There is really only one record. When you change that single record—whether as part of a group or as part of the database—you update it.

Creating a New Group

Groups are useful when you want to work with a subset of your contact records. For example, you may be planning a promotion for several of your contacts. You can group all the promotion contacts together and then work with the group.

To create a new group, follow these steps:

1. If you want to start with a lookup group, create the lookup group. Lookups are covered in Lesson 7.

2. Open the View menu and select the Edit Groups command. ACT! displays the Edit Groups dialog box (see Figure 8.1 below).

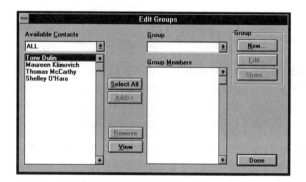

Figure 8.1 Creating a group.

3. Click on the New button. ACT! displays the New Group dialog box (see Figure 8.2 below).

Figure 8.2 Type the new group name.

4. In the Name text box, type a name for the group. This name will be displayed in the list of available groups.

5. In the Description text box, type a description of the group. Use this description as a reminder of the group's purpose.

6. Click on the OK button. ACT! creates the new group.

The group name appears in the Group text box in the Edit Groups dialog box. The next step is to assign contacts to this group.

Adding Contacts to a Group

Once you have created and named a group, you can assign contacts to that group. You can select contacts from the current lookup, from another group, or from a list of all contacts. To add contacts to a group, follow these steps:

1. In the Edit Groups dialog box, display the Available Contacts drop-down list. This list includes Current Lookup, ALL, and the groups you have created already.

2. Select which list of available contacts you want to use. When you make a selection, ACT! displays a list of contacts in that group or lookup. If you want to select from any contact in the database, select ALL. If you want to start with a shorter list, create a lookup and then select Current Lookup for Available Contacts.

3. To add contacts from the list of available contacts to the list of group members:

> **To add all available contacts,** first click on a single name in the list and then click on the Select All button. Next click on the Add button to include all the selected names in the Group Members list.

> OR

To add a single contact, click on the name and then click on the Add button. Do this for each contact you want to add. Figure 8.3 shows selected contacts added to the Group members list.

OR

To add several contacts: If they are contiguous, click on the first contact name and then hold down the Shift key and click on the last contact name. ACT! selects all contacts in between, including the first and last selected. If they are non-contiguous, click on the first contact name, hold down the Ctrl key, and then click on each contact name that you want to select.

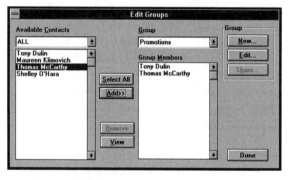

Figure 8.3   Adding contacts to the group.

4. When all the contacts you want are included in the Group Members list, click on the Done button. ACT! closes the dialog box and returns you to the contact screen.

Displaying a Group

The purpose of creating a group is so you can quickly display and work with contacts within a certain group. For example, suppose you grouped all your contacts for which a special promotion was planned. You can display this group of contacts by following these steps:

1. Open the View menu and select the Groups command. ACT! displays the View Group dialog box, which lists all the available groups (see Figure 8.4 below).

Figure 8.4 Viewing a group.

2. Click on the group you want to display.

3. Click on the OK button. ACT! groups and displays all contacts in the selected group. The status bar reminds you that you are viewing a subset of records or groups. The name of the group appears under the **Group** indicator.

Once you create and view the group, you can work with this subset of records. You can scroll through them without looking through the entire group of records. You can also delete a group, or edit all records in a group, as described in Lesson 6. If you do a lookup, only the records in the group are included in the lookup.

To return to the group of all records, follow these steps:

1. Open the View menu and select the Groups command.

2. Click on ALL as the group.

3. Click on the OK button.

Editing a Group

The members of a group aren't frozen. That is, you can easily add new members to a group or remove members from the group as needed. To do so, you simply edit the group by following these steps:

1. Open the View menu and select the Edit Groups command. ACT! displays the Edit Groups dialog box.

2. Display the Group drop-down list and select the group you want to change. ACT! displays the group name and the group members in the dialog box. You can change the name, the description, or the group members.

3. To change the name or description for the group, click on the Edit button. ACT! displays the Edit Group dialog box, which is similar to the New Group dialog box. Type a new name and description, and click on the OK button.

4. To change which contacts are members of the group, do any of the following:

   To add new members to the group, display the Available Contacts drop-down list, and select the group of contacts from which you want to choose. Then select the contacts you want to add, and click on the Add button to add them to the group.

   To remove members from the group, click on the name you want to remove in the Group Members list. Then click on the Remove button; click on Yes to confirm the removal. ACT! removes the name.

5. When you are finished making changes, click on the Done button. ACT! returns you to the contact screen.

Deleting a Group

If you have created a group by mistake, or no longer need a group, you can delete it. Keep in mind that you simply delete the group; you do not delete any of the contacts in that group. (For information about deleting the records in a group, see Lesson 6.)

Follow these steps to delete a group:

1. Open the View menu and select the Edit Groups command. ACT! displays the Edit Groups dialog box.

2. Display the Group drop-down list, and select the group you want to delete. ACT! displays the group name and the group members in the dialog box.

3. Click on the Edit button. ACT! displays the Edit Group dialog box.

4. Click on the Delete button. ACT! prompts you to confirm the deletion.

5. Click on the Yes button. ACT! deletes the group.

In this lesson you learned how to create groups of contacts; Lesson 9 teaches you how to view different layouts and create contact reports.

Lesson

Layouts and Contact Reports

In this lesson, you learn how to view contacts using differ-ent layouts, how to sort contacts, and how to create contact reports (such as an address book).

Viewing Contact Information

You can view different sets of fields for a contact (called *layouts*), and you can view a list of contacts (*contact list*), as described in this section.

Using Different Layouts

When you use the default contact layout, you have two screens full of information. If you want all the information at once, these two screens are handy. If you want to view just specific information, you may want to change the layout so that only some fields are displayed. For example, you may want to view the last contact(s) you had—last results, last call, last meeting, last letter, etc. In this case, you can use the historical layout. In addition to the Contact 1 and Contact 2 screens, ACT! provides eight other layouts you can use.

To change the layout, follow these steps:

1. Open the View menu and select the Layout com-mand. You see a submenu of choices.

2. Select the layout you want: Figure 9.1 shows the Alternate layout.

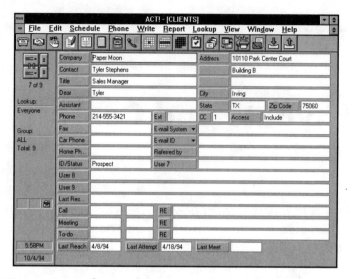

Figure 9.1   Alternate layout.

3. (Optional) To return to the previous layout, open the View menu and select the Layout command. From the submenu that appears, select the Previous command.

> **Keyboard Shortcut**   Press F6 to return to the previous layout.

Viewing a Contact List

When you use ACT!, you usually see one contact at a time. There may be instances when you want to view information about several contacts. For example, you can view a contact list with all the company names, contacts, states, and phone numbers for your contacts.

Follow these steps to display a contact list:

1. To display a list of everyone in the database, select the Lookup Everyone command.

I Don't Want Everyone! If you want to display a list of only some contacts, create a lookup group for the records you want displayed, as covered in Lesson 7.

2. Open the View menu and select the Contact List command. You see a contact list on-screen (see Figure 9.2 below).

Name	Contact	State	Phone	Tag
Corporate Image Products	Chris Huffman	TX	214-555-9665	+
Express Office Supply	Tim Kelly	TX	214-555-4909	+
Irvine Card Stock	David Ashley	CA	415-555-4590	+
Jordon Office Equipment	Jean Willis	TX	214-555-1098	+
National Paper	Janice Corben	NY	212-555-6756	+
OK Office Supply	Jeff Nelson	TX	214-555-0023	+
Paper Moon	Tyler Stephens	TX	214-555-3421	+
Papers Plus	Sean O'Hara	IN		+
Pop Printing	David Rechs	WA	813-555-6281	+

| Tag | Untag | Tag All | Untag All | | OK | Cancel |

Figure 9.2   A contact list.

Keyboard Shortcut   Press F8 to view a contact list.

3. When you are finished viewing the contact list, click on the OK button to close it.

Group Contacts   You can group contacts using the contact list. By default, all contacts are "tagged" or included in the group. To untag a contact, select it and then click on the Untag button. To untag all contacts, click on the Untag All button. You can then select the ones you want to include and click on the Tag button.

Sorting Contacts

By default, ACT! sorts the contacts in alphabetical order, on the basis of the company field. If you have two contacts with the same company name, ACT! sorts next on the last name, and then on the first name. You can sort the contacts in a different order by using a lookup. To do so, follow these steps:

1. Open the Lookup menu and select the field on which you want to sort: Company, First Name, Last Name, City, State, Zip Code, ID/Status.

2. In the dialog box that appears, press Backspace to delete any entries.

3. Click on the OK button. ACT! sorts the records, first by the lookup field and then by two additional fields.

Printing Contact Reports

In addition to changing the view of records, you can create printed reports. For example, you can print out an address book with address and phone information for your contacts. This section covers contact reports; ACT! also includes activity reports, which are covered in Lesson 13.

Printing an Address Book

The most common type of report is an *address book*. Being able to print an updated list of addresses will save you from scratching out and rewriting numbers. As long as your contact information is up to date, you can print an up-to-date address list.

Follow these steps to print an address book:

1. Open the Report menu and select the Print Address Book command. You see the ACT! Printouts dialog box (see Figure 9.3 on the following page).

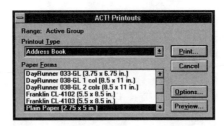

Figure 9.3 The ACT! Printouts dialog box.

2. If you want to print on a different type of paper, select the type of paper you want to use from the Paper Forms list.

3. If you want to see a preview of the report, check the Preview button (see Figure 9.4 below). Click on the Done button when you are finished looking at the preview.

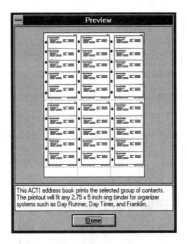

Figure 9.4 A preview of the report.

4. Click on the Print button. ACT! displays the Print dialog box (see Figure 9.5 on the following page).

5. Click on the OK button. ACT! prints the address book.

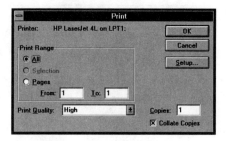

Figure 9.5   The Print dialog box.

You can customize the printout—select which fields
are included, select a sort order, change the font, and select
which contacts are included. To do so, click on the Options
button in the ACT! Printouts dialog box, and make your
selections. For more information, see your ACT! manual.

Creating Other Contact Reports

In addition to the address book, you can display and print
other contact reports—including a status report, a contact
report, a directory, and a phone list. To create and print this
type of report, follow these steps:

1. Open the Report menu and select the type of report
you want to create. ACT! displays the Prepare
Report dialog box (see Figure 9.6 below). Here you
select which contacts you want to include and
where to send the report.

Figure 9.6   The Prepare Report dialog box.

Is It Covered?   This section covers the Status Report, Contact Report, Directory, and Phone report. For information on creating the other reports, see Lesson 14.

2. In the Use area, select which contacts you want to include. You can include only the active contact, all contacts in the active lookup, or all contacts.

3. In the Output area, select where you want to send the report—to the printer, to a document, or over e-mail.

Which One's Best?   It's usually a good idea to send the report to a document. That way you can make any desired changes; once you have done so, you can print from the document screen. These steps assume you are creating a document.

4. Select Document, and then click on the OK button. ACT! displays the report on-screen in a word processing window (see Figure 9.7 on the following page).

5. To print the report, open the File menu and select the Print command. You see the Print dialog box.

6. Click on the OK button. ACT! prints the report.

Once you have a document on-screen (at step 4), you can edit it, make formatting changes, check spelling, and use any of the other word processing features. Lessons 15–20 cover the word processing program.

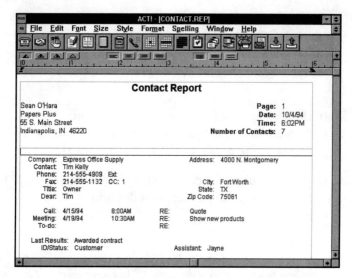

Figure 9.7 A contact report displayed as a word processing document.

In this lesson you learned how to view different contact layouts and create layout reports; Lesson 10 covers how to schedule calls.

Scheduling and Making Calls

In this lesson, you learn how to schedule a call, make a call, and time a call.

Scheduling a Call

For salespeople and other business professionals, phone calls are an important part of the day. ACT! makes it easy to remember who you have to call and track what calls you have made. You also can schedule calls, as described in this section.

To schedule a call, follow these steps:

1. Display the contact that you want to call. (Scroll through the records, or use the Lookup command).

2. Open the Schedule menu and select the Call command, or click on the Schedule call button. A calendar appears, and behind it, a dialog box (see Figure 10.1 on the following page).

3. Click on the date on which you want to make the call. (Use the scroll arrows in the calendar to change the month or year if needed).

4. Click on the OK button. ACT! next displays a date book so that you can select the time for the call (see Figure 10.2 on the following page).

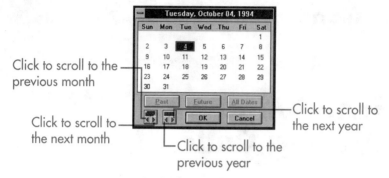

Click to scroll to the previous month

Click to scroll to the next month

Click to scroll to the next year

Click to scroll to the previous year

Figure 10.1   Scheduling a call.

Figure 10.2   Scheduling a time for the call.

5. Click on the time for the call, or drag across a time block to select a longer amount of time. Use the scroll arrows in the Day Book dialog box to select a time earlier or later than the ones shown.

Whenever...   If you can make the call at any time, click on the Timeless button.

6. Click on the OK button. ACT! next displays the RE dialog box (see Figure 10.3 below).

Figure 10.3 Enter the purpose of the call.

7. To select a purpose from the list, click on it and then choose OK. To enter a different purpose, click on Cancel, and type the purpose in the Regarding text box.

8. ACT! displays the Schedule an Activity dialog box (see Figure 10.4 on the following page). To accept the defaults, click on the OK button, or make any of the following changes first:

- To change the priority of the call, display the drop-down list and select a new priority.

- To set an alarm, or send your contact an e-mail message with the call information, check (respectively) the Set Alarm check box or the Send E-mail check box.

- To enter a lead time for the call, type the time in the Lead Time text box. You can press F2 to display the Lead Time popup.

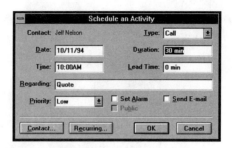

Figure 10.4 A scheduled call.

ACT! schedules the call, makes an entry in the activity list, displays an icon on the contract record, and enters the key call information in the Call fields on the contact screen.

On the day of the scheduled call, ACT! will remind you of the call in the calendars and activity reports for that day. If you have set an alarm, ACT! will remind you. (Lesson 12 covers managing scheduled activities.)

> **Schedule from Contact Screen** You can also use the Call fields in the contact screen to schedule a call. Type the entries that specify date, time, and what the message regards—or use the popup menus for these fields to make the entries.

Having ACT! Dial for You

When it comes time to make the call, you can display the contact screen and dial using the phone numbers displayed on-screen. If you have a modem that also functions as a phone, you can use the Phone menu to make the call.

To have ACT! dial for you, do the following:

1. Open the Phone menu and select the type of call you want to make—Local, Long Distance,

International, or Alternate Access (use a special long distance service or number). ACT! calls the contact's primary phone number.

Call Another Number   You can also dial another number. Open the Phone menu and select the List command, or click on the Phone List icon. ACT! displays a list of all numbers for the contact. Click on the number you want to call, or type the number in the Enter manually text box. Then click on the OK button.

2. Pick up the handset and click on the OK button. ACT! displays the Phone dialog box.

3. Do any of the following:

   To make a note in the contact history that the call was completed, click on the Yes button.

   To make a note that the call was attempted, click on the Attempted button.

   To redial the phone, click on the Redial button.

   To time the call, click on the Timer button. Timing a call is covered later in this lesson.

   To change the reason for the call, click on the Popup button. You see a list of Regarding topics; select the one you want and click on the OK button.

   To cancel the call, click on the Cancel button.

Phone Menu Options Don't Work
Remember that to use the Phone commands, you
must have a modem installed and set up. You also
must have a handset attached to the modem line.
You cannot use these commands if you don't have a
modem, the modem isn't set up, or you don't have a
handset. You also cannot use the Phone commands if
you have a PBX phone system.

Timing a Call

If you need to keep track of how long you talk to a contact,
you can use ACT!'s timer to do so. For instance, if you are a
consultant and bill by the time you spend, you can time a
call, meeting, or activity.

To time an activity, follow these steps:

1. Open the Edit menu and select the Start Timer
command. ACT! displays the Timer dialog box.

Keyboard Shortcut   Press Shift+F4 to start
the timer.

2. Select what you want to time—Call, Meeting, To-do,
or Other.

3. In the RE text box, type a note to remind yourself
what activity you are timing, or click on the Popup
button, select an item to specify what the message
regards, and click on the OK button.

4. Click on the OK button. ACT! displays the Elapsed
Time dialog box at the bottom of the contact screen
(see Figure 10.5 on the following page).

5. **(Optional)** You can pause the timer by clicking on the Pause button; click on the Restart button to restart the timer.

Figure 10.5 Timing a call.

6. When you are finished timing the call, click on the Stop button. ACT! records the time of the call as part of the contact history.

In this lesson you learned how to schedule and place a call; Lesson 11 covers how to schedule meetings and to-do activities.

Lesson

Scheduling Meetings and To-Do Activities

In this lesson, you learn how to schedule meetings and to-do items (such as sending a follow-up letter or making a presentation).

Scheduling a Meeting

In Lesson 10 you learned how to schedule a call. You can also use ACT! to schedule meetings. You follow the same basic steps: select the contact, choose the command, select a date, time, duration, etc. Here are the steps:

1. Display the contact with which you are meeting. (You can scroll through the records or use the Lookup command).

2. Open the Schedule menu and select the Meeting command, or click on the Meeting button. ACT! displays an on-screen calendar, with a dialog box behind the calendar (see Figure 11.1 on the following page).

3. Click on the meeting date. Use the scroll buttons to change the month or year if needed.

4. Click on the OK button. Next you see a date book where you select the time for the meeting. Other scheduled items are listed on the date book.

Figure 11.1 Selecting a date for the meeting.

5. Drag across the time for the meeting. For example, to schedule a meeting from 2:00 p.m. to 4:00 p.m., drag from 2:00 to 4:00 so that this time block is highlighted (see Figure 11.2 below).

> **No Particular Time** If you can hold the meeting at any time, click on the Timeless button.

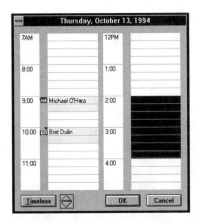

Figure 11.2 Scheduling a time for the meeting.

6. Click on the OK button. ACT! displays a popup box listing items that specify what the message regards (see Figure 11.3 on the following page).

Figure 11.3   Selecting the purpose of the meeting.

7. Click on the purpose and then click on the OK button; or, to enter a different purpose, click on Cancel and then type the purpose in the Regarding text box.

> **I Don't Like the Popup Choices!**   Remember that you can edit the popup menus, as described in Lesson 5.

8. To change the default priority, lead time, or alarm settings, click on the appropriate options in the dialog box.

9. Click on the OK button.

ACT! schedules the meeting, makes entries in the calendar and task list, and displays the meeting information on the contract screen (see Figure 11.4 on the following page).

> **Schedule Conflict**   When you display your date book and select a time, ACT! shows other calls, meetings, and to-do items for that day. If you select the same time for another activity, ACT! will display the Conflict dialog box. You can click on the Accept button to accept the conflict (both events are then scheduled for the same time), or click on the Reschedule button and select another date or time.

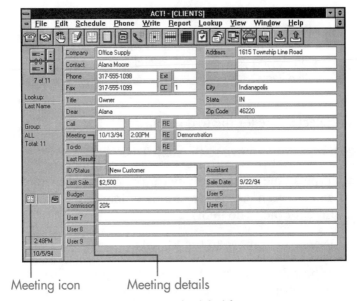

Meeting icon   Meeting details

Figure 11.4   A meeting scheduled for a contact.

Scheduling a To-Do Activity

You can use ACT! to schedule activities that you want to accomplish during the day. For instance, perhaps you have to complete a quote for a client or send a follow-up letter.

You can schedule an activity just like you schedule a call or meeting. Open the Schedule menu, select the To-do command, select a date, time, and purpose for the meeting, make any changes to the other schedule entries, and click on the OK button. (Refer to the preceding section for complete steps.)

Alternatively, you can schedule to-do activities (and calls and meetings) from the contact screen. The following steps explain how:

1. Display the contact with which you are meeting.

2. Click in the To-do field and press F2. ACT! displays a popup calendar.

Scheduling Activities That Don't Relate to a Particular Contact   You can schedule an activity not related to someone in your database by displaying your own record and then scheduling the item.

3. Select a date for the to-do item.

4. Press Tab to move to the next To-do field.

5. Type a time for the activity (or press F2 to display an on-screen date book, and then drag across the time for the to-do item).

6. Press Tab to move to the RE field.

7. Type a description of the activity (or press F2 to display a popup, and then select an item). Click on OK (see Figure 11.5 below). ACT! schedules the meeting.

The other entries that you can complete when you use the command method—lead time, priority, alarm settings, e-mail settings—are set to their default values.

Figure 11.5   A popup of to-do choices.

In this lesson you learned how to schedule meetings and to-do items; Lesson 12 explains how to manage your schedule.

Lesson

Managing Your Schedule

In this lesson, you learn how to manage your schedule—how to respond to an alarm, view calendars, and clear scheduled activities.

Setting Alarms to Remind You of Activities

One of the ways you can keep track of what activities you have scheduled is to set an alarm. Remember that to set an alarm, you check the Set Alarm check box in the Schedule an Activity dialog box. When it is time for that activity, ACT! beeps and displays the Critical Alarm dialog box (see Figure 12.1 below).

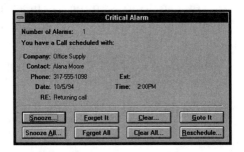

Figure 12.1 Responding to an alarm.

You can do any of the following:

- To display the contact for which the call or meeting is scheduled, click the Goto It button.

- To postpone the alarm, click on the Snooze button and then select the amount of time you want to postpone the alarm. To postpone all alerts, click on the Snooze All button and then select the amount of time in the Snooze dialog box.

- To forget the activity and alarm, click on the Forget It button. To forget all alerts, click on the Forget All button.

- To clear the activity, click on the Clear button. In the Clear Call or Clear Meeting dialog box that appears, select the option you want. (The section "Clearing Activities" covers clearing calls, meetings, and to-do items.) If you want to clear all activities, click on the Clear All button. Then select how you want to clear each activity.

- To reschedule the activity, click on the Reschedule button. Then schedule the activity for another date or time.

Viewing Calendars

Alarms work to remind you of individual meetings, calls, and activities, but you may prefer to view all the activities for the day, week, or year. You can do so with the calendar. You can also use the activity list and task list to view scheduled events; these options are covered in the next lesson.

To display a calendar view of your schedule, follow these steps:

1. Open the View menu. You see a submenu of choices.

2. Select Day to see a day view, Week to see a week view, and Month to see a month view of your calendar.

Figure 12.2 below shows a day view. You can use the buttons along the bottom of the calendar to move to another date, or to select a different view.

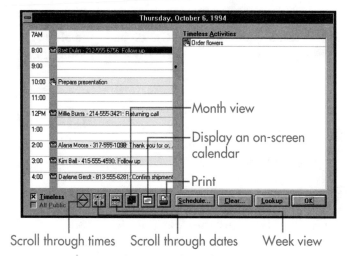

Month view

Display an on-screen calendar

Print

Scroll through times   Scroll through dates   Week view

Figure 12.2 A day view of a calendar.

Shortcuts You also can click on the Day View, Week View, or Month View buttons. Or you can press Shift+F5 for the day view, F3 for the week view, and F5 for the month view.

When the calendar you want is displayed, you can do any of the following:

- To move to the contact for which an activity is scheduled, double-click on the activity. ACT! displays the contact screen.

- To create a lookup group of all contacts with scheduled activities in that day, week, or month, click on the Lookup button. You then have a set of contacts for that particular time frame. You can move easily from one contact to the next, and then make any updates to the records.

- To clear an item, click on it and then click on the Clear button. (See the section "Clearing Activities" below for more information on clearing a call, meeting, or to-do item.)

- To reschedule an activity, click on it and then click on the Schedule button. ACT! displays the Modify an Activity dialog box. Make any changes and then click on OK.

> **Reschedule by Dragging** With a calendar on-screen, you can move an activity to another day or time by dragging it from its original spot to a new spot.

- To schedule a new activity, click on the day and time you want and then click on the Schedule button. ACT! displays the Schedule an Activity dialog box. You can select a different contact by clicking on the Contact button. You can change the item by displaying the Type drop-down list. Make any other entries and then click on the OK button.

Clearing Activities

Keeping track of what calls, meetings, and to-do items you have to complete is only half of the schedule information you need. You also will want to keep track of what calls you made, what calls you attempted, which meetings were held, and which to-do items were completed. You should use ACT! not only to schedule the call but also to enter the results of the call, meeting, or to-do item, as described in this section.

Clearing Calls

You can use two methods to clear a call. With the Clear command, ACT! clears the call from the activity list and makes an entry to the contact history. When you use the Call

History command, ACT! makes an entry to the contact history as well, but does not clear the call from the schedule. Depending on whether or not you want to keep the call scheduled, you will use one command or the other.

To clear a call so it is no longer listed in your activity and calendars, follow these steps:

1. Open the Schedule menu and select the Clear command. You see a submenu of choices.

2. Select the Call command. ACT! displays the Clear Call dialog box (see Figure 12.3 below).

Figure 12.3 Clearing a call.

3. Do one of the following:

   To record the call as completed in the contact history—and clear the call—click on the Completed Call option.

   To make a record in the contact history that the call was attempted, and to clear the scheduled call, click on the Attempted Call option.

   If you received the call and want to clear it from the schedule, click on the Received Call option.

   If you left a message and want to clear the call from the schedule, click on the Left Message option.

To erase the call from the schedule without
making an entry in the contact history, click on
the Erase Call option.

4. Click on the OK button. The appropriate entry
appears in the contact history. ACT! deletes the call
from the activity list, and updates the Last Reach
and Last Attempt dates as appropriate.

If you want to keep the call scheduled, but make notes
in the contact history of your call attempts, follow these
steps:

1. Open the Phone menu and select the Call History
command. ACT! displays the Call History dialog box
(see Figure 12.4 below).

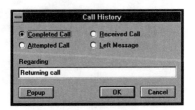

Figure 12.4 Keeping a call history.

2. Select the appropriate option: Completed Call,
Attempted Call, Received Call, or Left Message.

What's the Difference? Remember that the
difference between keeping a call history and
clearing a call is that when you follow these
steps, ACT! retains the scheduled call on the
calendar and activity lists.

3. Click on the OK button.

ACT! makes the appropriate entry in the contact history. (Contact histories are covered in Lesson 13.)

Clearing a Meeting

In addition to clearing calls, you should also clear the meetings from the schedule. To do so, follow these steps:

1. Display the contact for which you want to clear the meeting. ACT! will clear the meeting that is listed on the contact screen.

> **More Than One?** If you have more than one meeting scheduled and want to clear a different meeting, use the activity list to clear it (see Lesson 13).

2. Open the Schedule menu and select the Clear Meeting command. You see a prompt that asks you whether the meeting was held.

3. Click on the Yes button. ACT! clears the meeting from the activity list, makes an entry in the contact history, and updates the Last Meet date.

Clearing an Activity

You can also clear activities that were completed by following these steps:

1. Display the contact for which the item was scheduled. ACT! will clear the current to-do item.

2. Open the Schedule menu and select the Clear To-do command. You see a message asking whether the to-do item was completed.

3. Click on the Yes button. ACT! clears the activity from the activity list and makes an entry in the contact history.

   In this lesson you learned how to set and respond to alarms, view and work with calendars, and clear activities; Lesson 13 explains how to work with the task list, activity list, and contact history.

Lesson 13

Using the Task List, Activity List, and Contact History

In this lesson, you learn how to use the task list, activity list, and contact history.

Using the Task List

As you learned in Lesson 12, you can use a calendar to display the activities for a particular day, week, or month. In addition to using this method to view scheduled activities, you can use the *task list*. This list displays calls, meetings, and to-do items for the current date, a future date, or a range of dates.

You can customize the list to display just what you want. For example, you can display only high-priority tasks in the task list. You can also update the task list—for instance, reschedule or clear an activity.

Displaying the Task List

When you display the task list, you see the schedule tasks for the current day (see Figure 13.1 on the following page). You can change which day's activities are displayed, and what types of activities are displayed. To display the task list, follow these steps:

1. Open the View menu and select the Task List command, or click on the View Task List button.

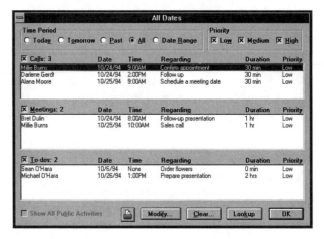

Figure 13.1   A task list.

Keyboard Shortcut   Press F7 to display the task list.

2. If you want to display another day's activities, do one of the following:

To view the activities for tomorrow, click on the Tomorrow option button.

To view all past activities, click on the Past option button.

To view all activities, click on the All option button.

To view activities for a range of dates, click on the Date Range option button. ACT! displays an on-screen calendar. Drag across the dates you want to include in the task list, or click on one of the command buttons (Past, Future, All Dates) to include those dates. Click on the OK button.

3. To change which activities are displayed, click in the Calls, Meetings, or To-dos check box. Marked activities will be included in the task list; unmarked activities will be omitted.

4. Check which priorities you want to include in the task list: Low, Medium, or High.

> **Look up by Priority**   You can do a priority lookup to look up tasks of a certain priority. Open the Lookup menu and select the Priority command. Check which priority to include, click on the OK button, select a date range, and click OK again.

5. When you are finished viewing the task list, click on the OK button. ACT! displays the contact screen.

For information on printing the task list, see Lesson 14.

Updating the Task List

When the task list is on-screen, you can update it (create a lookup group, modify a scheduled activity, etc.) by using the command buttons along the bottom of the window.

To reschedule or clear an item, follow these steps:

1. Click on the item you want to modify.

2. Do one of the following:

> **To reschedule or change an activity**, click on the Modify button. Make any changes to the type of activity, date, time, duration, lead time, priority, and purpose; then click on the OK button.

> **To clear an item**, click on the Clear button. Make the appropriate choice in the dialog box. Lesson 14 explains how to clear an item.

> **To create a lookup group** of all the contacts listed in the task list, click on the Lookup button.

3. Click on the OK button to close the task list.

Using the Activity List

In some cases, you may not be interested in the big picture—all the activities for a particular day. Instead, you may want to see just the activities for a selected contact. For example, suppose you have a meeting scheduled next week with a customer, and you have scheduled several other activities before that meeting. You can review the activity list for that contact to see all the scheduled tasks.

If you want to view the activities you have already completed for the contact, view the contact history, as described in the next section.

To display the activity list, follow these steps:

1. Display the contact you want.

2. Open the View menu and select the Activities command or click on the Activities icon. ACT! displays the activity list for the contact (see Figure 13.2 below).

Figure 13.2 An activity list.

Keyboard Shortcut   Press Alt+F9 to display the activity list.

3. Click on the Add button to add new activities, the Modify button to change an activity, and the Clear button to clear an activity.

4. After you finish reviewing the activities, click on the OK button to close the window.

To view the total number of activities performed for the contact, open the View menu and select the Totals command, or press Ctrl+F9. ACT! displays the total number of calls completed, calls attempted, meetings held, and letters sent (see Figure 13.3).

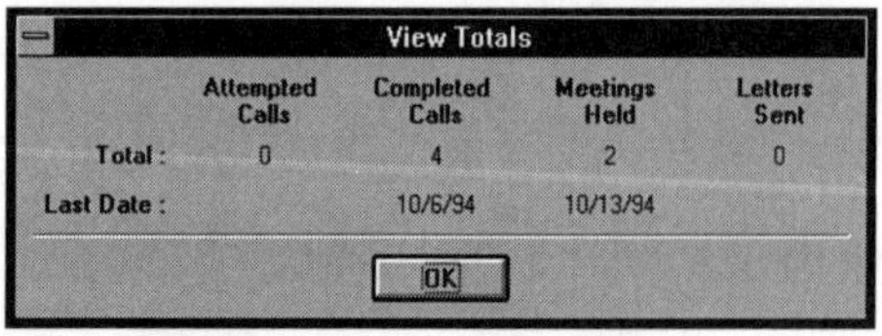

View Totals				
	Attempted Calls	Completed Calls	Meetings Held	Letters Sent
Total :	0	4	2	0
Last Date :		10/6/94	10/13/94	

OK

Figure 13.3   Viewing activity totals.

Using the Contact History

The activity list displays scheduled activities that you have not yet cleared. What if you want to view past activities? To do this, you use the contact history. The *contact history* is a record of your calls, meetings, and projects with a contact. You can use this information to remind yourself what has transpired between you and the contact.

To display the contact history, follow these steps:

1. Display the contact whose history you want to see.

2. Open the View menu and select the History command, or click on the History icon. ACT! displays the date, time, and type of event that was scheduled and completed for the contact (see Figure 13.4 below).

		History for Alana Moore	
Date	**Time**	**Type**	**Event**
10/13/94	2:00PM	Meeting Held	Demonstration
10/12/94	9:00AM	To-do Done	
10/6/94	2:00PM	Completed Call	Thank you for order
10/5/94	2:56PM	Left Message	Returning call
10/5/94	2:50PM	Completed Call	Returning call
10/5/94	2:00PM	Completed Call	Returning call
9/16/94	None	To-do Done	Send catalog
9/15/94	10:00AM	Meeting Held	Sales Presentation
9/12/94	9:00AM	Completed Call	Introductory call

☐ Show All Public History   [Update] [Remove...] [OK]

Figure 13.4 A contact history.

Keyboard Shortcut Press Shift+F9 to display the contact history.

3. If you need to remove events from the history, click on the event you want to delete; then click on the Remove button. Confirm the change by clicking on the Yes button when prompted.

4. Click on the OK button to close the contact history.

In this lesson you learned how to view different lists of activities; in Lesson 14, you learn how to create reports of activities.

Lesson

Activity Reports

In this lesson, you learn how to print a calendar, as well as how to view and print activity reports.

Printing a Calendar

If you are traveling, you may not have access to your computer, and therefore your list of scheduled activities. In this case, you may want to print a copy of your calendar to take with you. You can print a daily, weekly, or monthly calendar on plain or day-planner-type paper.

To print a calendar, follow these steps:

1. Open the Report menu and select the Print Calendar command. The ACT! Printouts dialog box appears (see Figure 14.1 below).

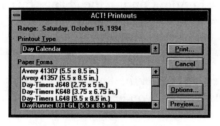

Figure 14.1 Printing a calendar.

2. By default, ACT! displays a daily calendar. If you want to print a weekly or monthly calendar, open the Printout Type drop-down list and select the type of calendar you want to print.

3. In the Paper Forms list, select a paper type. You can select one and then click on the Preview button to see what the paper looks like. Figure 14.2 shows a preview of one of the Day Runner paper types.

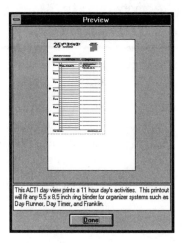

This ACT! day view prints a 11 hour day's activities. This printout will fit any 5.5 x 8.5 inch ring binder for organizer systems such as Day Runner, Day Timer, and Franklin.

Done

Figure 14.2 A preview of a calendar using Day Runner as the paper form type.

Customize the Calendar You can control which activities are included in the calendar, what starting time is used, and other options by clicking the Options button, making your selections, and clicking the OK button.

4. Click on the Print button. ACT! displays the Print dialog box.

5. To print the calendar, click on the OK button.

Viewing and Printing Activity Reports

In addition to calendars, you can display and print other types of activity reports. The following table describes each

of the available reports. Note: Lesson 9 covers contact
reports (Status Report, Contact Report, Directory, and
Phone).

Table 14.1 Activity reports.

Type of Report	Description
Activities Completed	Prints a list of all completed activities.
History Summary	Prints a summary of a contact's history (attempted calls, completed calls, meetings held, and letters sent).
Future Activity	Prints a list of all future activities.
Task List	Prints a task list (calls, meetings, and to-do items).
Notes	Prints the notes for all selected contacts.

To create a report, follow these steps:

1. Open the Report menu. You see a list of predefined reports.

2. Select the type of report you want: Activities Completed, History Summary, Future Activity, Task List, or Notes.

3. Skip to step 5 if you selected Future Activity. Otherwise, do one of the following to select the dates to include from the calendar that appears (see Figure 14.3 on the following page):

   To include all past dates, click on the Past button.

To include all future dates, click on the Future button.

To include all dates, click on the All Dates button.

To include a range of dates, click and hold down the mouse button on the first date; then drag across the dates you want to include.

Figure 14.3   Selecting the dates to include.

4. Click on the OK button. ACT displays the Prepare Report dialog box (see Figure 14.4 below). Here you can select where to send the report and which contacts to include.

Figure 14.4   Selecting the contacts to include and where to send the report.

5. To select which contacts to include, do one of the following:

To include only the active contact, select the
Active Contact option.

To include all contacts in the active lookup,
select the Active Lookup option.

To include all contacts, select the All Contacts
option.

Only One Option   When you choose the Task
List, the only option available is All Contacts.

6. To select where to send the report, do one of the
following:

To create a word processing document which
you can view, edit, and print, select Document.
Figure 14.5 below shows a Completed Activity
Report.

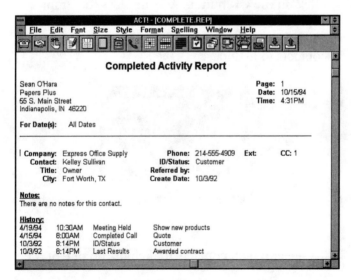

Figure 14.5   A report displayed as a word processing
document.

To send the report directly to the printer, select
Printer.

To send the report over e-mail, select E-mail.

7. Click on the OK button. ACT! prints or displays the
report, depending on what you selected for step 6.

If you created a document, you can print the document
by opening the File menu and selecting the Print command.
Click on the OK button to complete the procedure.

In this lesson you learned how to create activity reports;
Lesson 15 explains the basics of using the word processing
features of ACT!

Lesson

Creating Documents

In this lesson, you learn how to create a document, type text, move around, select text, and delete text.

Creating a Document

The main part of ACT! is *contact management*—keeping track of people's names, addresses, and other information, as well as scheduling calls, meetings, and to-do items. As part of your contact management, you may need to communicate in written form—in a letter, memo, report, or other document type. ACT! includes a word processing program so you can create these types of documents.

To create a document, open a document window by following these steps:

1. Open the File and select the New command. ACT! displays the New File dialog box (see Figure 5.1 below).

Figure 15.1 Selecting the type of file you want to create.

2. Click on the Document button.

ACT! starts the word processing program; a blank word processing document appears on-screen (see Figure 15.2 below). You can then type the text of the document, as covered in the next section.

Toolbar —
Ruler —

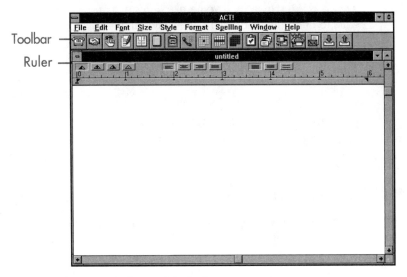

Figure 15.2.   A blank document.

Typing Text

You type text by pressing the letter and number keys on the keyboard. As you type, a flashing vertical line called the *insertion point* moves to the right. When you reach the end of the line, you don't have to press Enter. Just keep typing; ACT! will insert line breaks, as needed. This feature is known as *word wrap*, and enables you to add or delete text without retyping. If you add text, ACT! adjusts the lines accordingly to make room. If you delete text, ACT! moves text up to fill in the gap.

When to Press Enter   You should press Enter only when you want to end a paragraph or insert a blank line.

ACT! also inserts page breaks as needed. If you need to force a page break, press Shift+Enter (or open the Format menu and select the Insert Page Break command).

Make a Mistake? If you make a mistake and want to delete the character you just typed, press Backspace. Backspacing deletes characters to the left of the insertion point. Pressing Delete deletes characters to the right of the insertion point.

Keep in mind that the document is stored only temporarily in the computer's memory. To learn how to save a permanent copy of the document, see Lesson 18.

Moving Around the Document

The insertion point indicates where text will be inserted when you type. When you want to add text somewhere else in the document, move the insertion point to that spot.

You can use the mouse or the keyboard to move around the document. To use the mouse, point to where you want to place the insertion point and click the mouse button. The insertion point jumps to that spot.

Table 15.1 lists the keyboard shortcuts you can use to move around the document.

Table 15.1 Movement keys.

To move	Press
One character right	→
One character left	←
One line up	↑
One line down	↓

To move	Press
Beginning of the line	Home
End of the line	End
Previous screen	PgUp
Next screen	PgDn
Top of the document	Ctrl+Home
End of the document	Ctrl+End
Top of screen	Ctrl+PgUp
Bottom of screen	Ctrl+PgDn

Selecting Text

Many of ACT!'s word processing features require you to
select the text you want to modify before you execute the
command. For example, to make text bold, you select the
text you want to change and then select the command for
bold. You also need to select text before you move, copy,
delete, or format it. Use either the mouse or the keyboard to
select.

To use the mouse to select text, follow these steps:

1. Click at the start of the text you want to select.

2. Hold down the mouse button and drag across the
   text you want to select.

3. Release the mouse button. The text appears in
   reverse video on-screen (see Figure 15.3 on the
   following page).

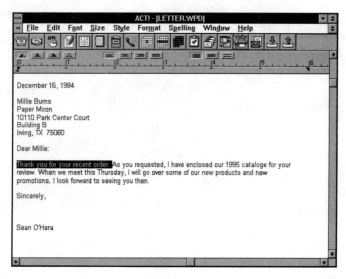

Figure 15.3   Selected text.

To use the keyboard to select text, follow these steps:

1. Move the insertion point to the start of the text you want to select.

2. Press and hold down the Shift key and use the cursor movement keys to highlight the text.

3. Release the Shift key.

> **Select All of the Text**   To select the entire document, open the Edit menu and click on the Select All command, or press Ctrl+A.

To deselect text, click outside the selected text (or release the Shift key and press any other key).

Adding and Deleting Text

To add text, just move the insertion point to where you want the new text to be and start typing. ACT! moves existing text over to make room for the new text.

As mentioned, you can delete a character with the Backspace or Delete keys. Backspace deletes characters to the left; Delete deletes characters to the right. If you have a lot of text to delete, it is easier to select the text first; then you can delete it all at once by pressing either Delete or Backspace. ACT! deletes the selected text, and moves up and over existing text to fill in the gap.

> **Undelete Text**   If you deleted text by accident, undo the deletion by opening the Edit menu and selecting the Undo command. Be sure to select this command *immediately* after the unintended deletion.

In this lesson you learned the basics of creating a new document and typing text; Lesson 16 introduces you to some additional editing features included in ACT!'s word processing program.

Lesson

Editing a Document

In this lesson, you learn about some of the editing features you can use to make changing a document easy. You learn how to move and copy text, how to find and replace text, and how to check your spelling.

Moving Text

Because your words, sentences, and paragraphs aren't committed to paper, but are merely displayed on-screen, you can easily rearrange the order of the text. You may want to move an idea up in the document, or rearrange the order of sentences in a paragraph so that they read better. To move text, first you *cut* it from the document, then you *paste* it back in at a new location. Follow these steps:

1. Select the text you want to move. (Lesson 15 covers selecting text.)

2. Open the Edit menu and select the Cut command. ACT! deletes the text from the document, storing it in a temporary holding location called the Clipboard.

> **Keyboard Shortcut** Press Ctrl+X to cut selected text. Press Ctrl+V to paste text you have cut or copied.

Clipboard   The Clipboard is a Windows feature that enables you to cut or copy text or graphics from one place to another. You can cut and paste from one location to another in the same document, from one document to another, or from one application to another.

3. Move the insertion point to where you want the cut text to appear.

4. Open the Edit menu and select the Paste command. ACT! pastes the cut text.

Copying Text

In addition to cutting and pasting text, you can also *copy* and paste text. The procedure is the same, except you use the Copy command instead of the Cut command. Copying text is useful if you need to repeat a block of information in the document or use the same information with minor changes.

To copy text, follow these steps:

1. Select the text that you want to copy.

2. Open the Edit menu and select the Copy command. ACT! copies the text to the Clipboard. Notice that the text remains in the document.

Keyboard Shortcut   Press Ctrl+C to copy selected text.

3. Use the mouse or the keyboard to move the insertion point to where you want to place the copy.

4. Open the Edit menu and select the Paste command. The copied text appears in the new location.

Finding Text

It is easy to scan a short document for a particular word or phrase. In a longer document, scanning to find the spot you want is time-consuming. Rather than look through page after page of text, you can have ACT! find a particular word or phrase for you.

1. Open the Edit menu and select the Find/Replace command. ACT! displays the Find/Replace dialog box (see Figure 16.1 below).

Type the word you want to find.

Figure 16.1   The Find/Replace dialog box.

2. In the Find What text box, type the word, phrase, or part of a word you want to find.

> **Be Specific!**   To get the best results, type something unique. If you type a phrase that occurs many times, you will have to search through all its occurrences to find the one you want. If you search for a unique phrase, you limit the search.

3. To find only whole words, check the Whole Word check box. This option helps limit your search.

> **Whole Word**   If you don't select this option, ACT! stops on the characters you enter, whether these characters are a word or part of a word. If you search for *act*, for example, ACT! will stop on *act*, char*act*er, p*act*, etc. When Whole Word is checked, ACT! will stop only on *act*.

4. To match the case as you have typed it, check the Case Sensitive check box. For example, if you check this and type ACT, the program will stop only on *ACT*—not on *act* or *Act*.

5. Click on the Find Next button. ACT! moves to and selects the first occurrence of the text. The dialog box remains open on-screen.

6. To move to the next occurrence, click on the Find Next button again. Do this until you move to the location you want. To close the dialog box, click on the Cancel button.

> **No Matches Found** If ACT! cannot find a match, it displays an error message. Click on the OK button and try the search again. Be sure you typed the text correctly. Be sure the options aren't limiting your search too much.

Replacing Text

The companion to Find is Replace. You can use this half of the command to search for a certain word or phrase and replace it with another word or phrase. For example, you could search for *ACT* and replace it with *ACT! for Windows*.

To search for and replace text, follow these steps:

1. Open the Edit menu and select the Find/Replace command. You see the Find/Replace dialog box.

2. In the Find What text box, type the text you want to find. For example, to search for and replace *ACT*, type **ACT**.

3. In the Replace With text box, type the text you want to use as the replacement. To use the text **ACT! for Windows** as a replacement, type that text.

4. Check the Whole Word or Case Sensitive check boxes, if needed.

5. Click on the Find Next button. ACT! moves to the first occurrence of the text and selects it (see Figure 16.2 below).

Found text

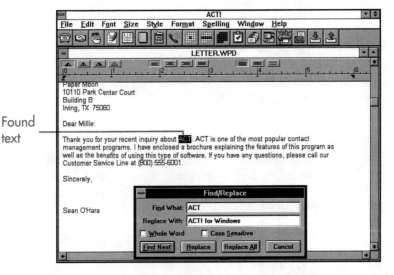

Figure 16.2 Searching for and replacing text.

6. Do one of the following for each instance ACT! flags:

> Click on the Find Next button to skip this occurrence and move to the next one.

> Click on the Replace button to make this replacement; then click the Find Next button to move to the next one.

> Click on the Replace All button to replace all occurrences.

7. When you reach the end of the document, click on the Cancel button to close the dialog box.

Checking Your Spelling

You can use the spelling program to check your spelling. Once you have used the speller, however, be sure you understand how this feature works before you become overconfident about the accuracy of your document.

The speller works by comparing the words in your document to the words in its dictionary. If ACT! cannot find the word, it flags it. This means two things. First, the word may not be misspelled; the speller may stop on your last name or first name, which may be spelled correctly, but just isn't in the dictionary. Second, the word may be spelled correctly but used incorrectly. ACT! doesn't know the meanings of *weather* and *whether* and when to use which; it only knows if the word is spelled correctly.

To check spelling, follow these steps:

1. Open the Spelling menu and select the Check Document command. ACT! starts the spell check, flagging any words it cannot find and displaying them in the Spell Check dialog box (see Figure 16.3 on the following page).

2. For each of the words ACT! stops on, do one of the following:

To skip this word and move to the next word, click on the Skip button. Use this button if the word is spelled correctly.

To add the word to your user dictionary, click on the Add button. Use this button for words you use frequently and don't want to have flagged—for example, your name.

Flagged word

```
┌─────────────────────────────────────────────────────────────┐
│ ═                              ACT!                      ▼ ♦ │
│ File  Edit  Font  Size  Style  Format  Spelling  Window  Help │
│ [toolbar icons]                                               │
│ ┌──────────────────────── LETTER.WPD ──────────────────── ▼ ▲┐
│ │ [ruler]                                                 │
│ │ Building B                                               │
│ │ Irving, TX 75060                                         │
│ │                                                          │
│ │ Dear Millie:                                             │
│ │                                                          │
│ │ Thank you for your recent inquiry about ACT. ACT is one of the most popular contact │
│ │ management programs. I have enclosed a brochure explaining the features of this program as │
│ │ well as the benefits of using this type of software. If you have any questions, please call our │
│ │ Customer Service Line at (800) 555-6001.                 │
│ │                                                          │
│ │ Sincerely,                                               │
│ │                     ┌──────────── Spell Check ──────────┐│
│ │                     │ ═                                  ││
│ │ Sean O'Hara         │ Word: beneilts      Suggestions:  ││
│ │                     │                     ┌───────────┐ ││
│ │                     │ Replace With:       │ benefice  │ ││
│ │                     │ ┌─────────────────┐ │ benefits  │ ││
│ │                     │ │ benefice        │ │ benefit   │ ││
│ │                     │ └─────────────────┘ │ benefit's │ ││
│ │                     │ ☒ Auto Suggest      └───────────┘ ││
│ │                     │ [Replace] [Skip] [Suggest] [Add] [Cancel] ││
│ └─────────────────────└────────────────────────────────────┘
└─────────────────────────────────────────────────────────────┘
```

Type word here...   or select word here

Figure 16.3 Checking your spelling.

If the word is misspelled and the correct spelling is listed in the Suggestions list, click on the correct spelling, and then click on the Replace button.

If the word is misspelled, but the correct spelling is not listed, type the correct spelling in the Replace With text box, and then click on the Replace button.

3. After all words are checked, you see a dialog box showing the number of words checked and the number of misspelled words found. Click on the OK button.

Speller Won't Run Open the Spelling menu and select the Choose Main Dictionary command. Select the dictionary ENGLISH.DCT in the ACTWIN2\SPELL directory. Click on the OK button.

Lesson

17

Saving, Opening, and Printing Documents

In this lesson, you learn how to save documents, open documents, and print documents.

Saving a Document

When you are typing text in a word processing document, that text is stored only temporarily in the computer's memory. To make a permanent copy, you will need to save the document to your hard disk. The first time you save a document, you are prompted to enter a file name.

After you save once, you aren't prompted for a file name when you save the same document again; instead, ACT! saves the document with the same name.

> **Be Safe!** If the power goes off, or your computer fails while you are working on a document, you will lose the changes you've made since the last time you saved that document. To be safe, re-save your document every five to ten minutes as you work.

Follow these steps to save a document.

1. Open the File menu and select the Save command. You see the Save dialog box (see Figure 17.1).

2. In the File Name text box, type a file name of up to eight characters. ACT! will use the extension **WPD** automatically for all word processing documents.

3. Click on the OK button.

> **Save It Where?** By default, ACT! stores all documents in the ACTWIN2\DOCS directory. To save the file to another directory, double-click on the directory name in the Directories list. To save the file to another drive, display the Drives drop-down list, and then click on the drive you want.

Type file name here ——

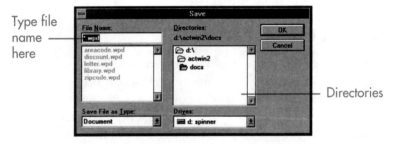

—— Directories

Figure 17.1   Saving a document.

> **Keyboard Shortcut!** Press Ctrl+S to save a document.

ACT! saves the document, and displays the file name in the title bar of the document window. To save the document again, simply select the File Save command again.

To save an existing document under a new name, open the File menu and select the Save As command. Type a new file name and click on the OK button.

Closing a Document

When you finish working on a document, you can close it and return to the contact screen. Open the File menu and select the Close command, or double-click on the Control-menu box for the window.

If you did not save the document, you are reminded to save. Click on the Yes button to save, the No button to close without saving, and the Cancel button to return to the document without saving.

Keyboard Shortcut Press Ctrl+W to close a document.

Opening a Document

In many cases, you will want to open a document you have previously saved.

Follow these steps:

1. Open the File menu and select the Open command. You see the Open File dialog box (see Figure 17.2).

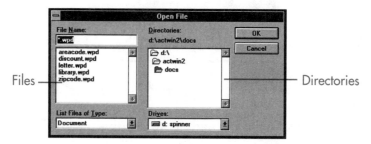

Files ——   —— Directories

Figure 17.2 Opening a document.

2. If necessary, display the List Files of Type drop-down list and select Document. ACT! displays the document files.

3. In the File Name list, select the file you want to open.

4. Click on the OK button. ACT! displays the document on-screen.

> **Keyboard Shortcuts!**   Press Ctrl+O to display the Open File dialog box.
>
> Press Shift+F11 to display the Print dialog box.

Printing a Document

The purpose of creating most documents is to print them so that you can share them with someone else. Follow these steps to print a document:

1. Open the File menu and select the Print command. ACT! displays the Print dialog box (see Figure 17.3).

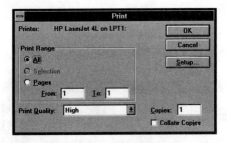

Figure 17.3   Printing a document.

2. Click on the OK button. ACT! prints the document.

In the Print dialog box, you can choose to print more than one copy, and/or print only certain pages of each copy. To print more than one copy, enter the number of copies in the Copies text box. To print a range of pages, choose the Pages option and enter the page range you want to print.

Lesson

Creating a Letter, Memo, or Fax

In this lesson, you learn how to create a letter, memo, or fax for any of the contacts in your database.

Creating a Letter

In Lessons 15-17, you learned how to create a blank document and type the text you wanted to include. You can also start the word processing program and create a blank letter with today's date; a contact's name, company, and address; a salutation; and closing. You can then type the body of the letter.

Follow these steps to create a letter.

1. Display the contact to which you want to send the letter. ACT! will use this record for the letter information (name and address).

2. Open the Write menu and select the Letter command. ACT! inserts the date, contact name and address, salutation, and closing (see Figure 18.1).

3. Click under the salutation and type the text of the letter.

4. Save the letter, as described in Lesson 17.

5. Open the File menu and select the Print command to print the letter. Click on OK.

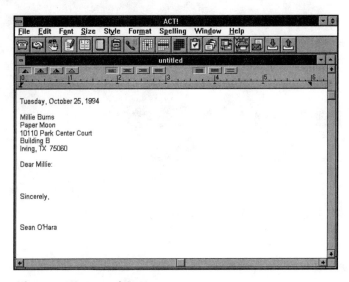

Figure 18.1 A letter.

6. A dialog box appears, asking whether this is a letter that will be sent out. Click on Yes if this is a finished letter; click on No if it is a rough draft.

> **What's the Difference?** In step 6, if you click on Yes, ACT! updates the **Letter Date** and **Letter Name** fields on the contact database screen. If you choose No, a draft is printed, but the fields are not updated.

7. When asked, click on Yes, and then OK to print an envelope, or click on No to skip the envelope.

ACT! prints the envelope if you requested it and updates the **Letter Date** and **Letter Name** fields, if necessary.

Creating a Memo

Another common type of document is a memo. You can
create a memo that will pull the contact name from the
current contact screen, enter a memo heading and the
current date, and insert your name—all automatically. To
create a memo, follow these steps:

1. Display the contact to which you want to send the
memo.

2. Open the Write menu and select the Memorandum
command. ACT! creates the memo (see Figure 18.2
below).

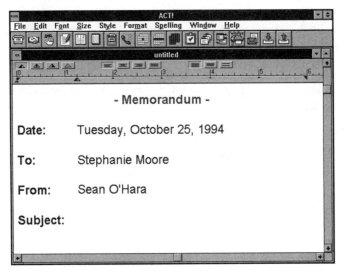

Figure 18.2 A memo.

3. Complete the memo.

4. Select the File Save command to save the memo.
(Saving is covered in more detail in Lesson 17.)

5. To print the memo, use the File, Print command, and then click on OK.

6. ACT! asks whether the document is one that will be sent out. Click on Yes if you plan to send the memo, or No if the memo is just a draft.

Clicking on Yes in step 6 updates the **Letter Date** and **Letter Name** fields on the contact database screen. Clicking on No does not update these fields.

Creating and Sending a Fax

ACT! also enables you to create a fax cover sheet, another common document type. ACT! will set up the fax cover sheet, insert the current date, and pull the contact name and fax number from the current contact. Follow these steps to create a fax cover sheet:

1. Display the contact to whom you want to send the fax.

2. Open the Write menu and select the Fax Cover command. You see the fax document on-screen (see Figure 18.3 on the following page).

3. Complete the fax.

4. Use the File, Save command to save the fax.

5. To print, select the File, Print command and then click on OK.

6. ACT! asks whether the document is one that will be sent out. Click on Yes if you plan to send the fax, or No if the fax is just a draft. ACT! prints the cover sheet.

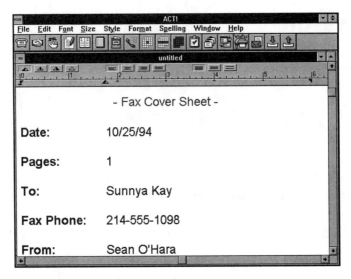

Figure 18.3 A fax cover sheet.

Clicking on Yes in step 6 updates the **Letter Date** and **Letter Name** fields on the contact database screen. Clicking on No does not make any changes to the contact screen.

> **FAX/Modem as Printer** To fax the document from your computer, your FAX/Modem must be selected as the current printer. From the Print dialog box, click on the Setup button. Then select the FAX/Modem as the printer. Click on OK twice to start printing. Follow the particular instructions for your fax modem.

In this lesson you learned how to create a letter, memo, or fax for a particular contact; Lesson 19 discusses some of the formatting features you can use in a document.

Lesson

Formatting Text

In this lesson, you learn about the different ways you can format text in a word processing document.

What Is a Font?

A *font* is a set of characters and numbers in a certain design. In your word processing documents, you can select a font that best conveys the message you want. For example, you may want a traditional font such as Times New Roman for a business proposal. For an invitation, you might want something more fun and imaginative. Figure 19.1 shows some examples of different fonts. Notice how each font has its own look.

What fonts you have available will depend on your printer and your computer system. Every printer comes with certain built-in fonts; you can use any of the fonts that came on your computer. In addition, you will have certain Windows or TrueType fonts.

TrueType   A Windows font technology that stores fonts in a file on your hard disk. When you want to print using that font, the computer sends the font information to the printer. You can purchase and install additional TrueType fonts in Windows.

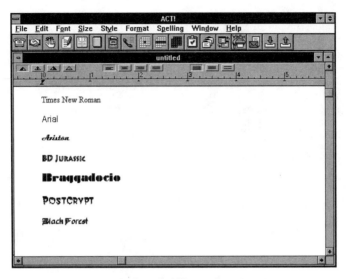

Figure 19.1 Examples of different fonts.

In addition to the different font names, you can select to change the style and size of the font, as described in this lesson.

Changing the Font Style

Bold, italic, and underline are common font styles, and can be easily applied to a word, phrase, or entire document. You may want to use a font style to make your text stand out. For example, you may want to boldface the name of your product in a letter.

To change the font style, follow these steps:

1. Select the text you want to change. Selecting text is covered in Lesson 15.

2. Open the Style menu to display a list of Style options (see Figure 19.2 on the following page). Click on the style you want.

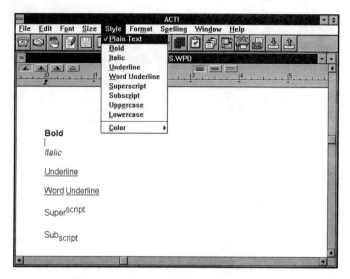

Figure 19.2 Selecting a font style.

(Note: You can also use the Style menu to change text from UPPERCASE to lowercase, or vice versa. This command is handy if you left the Caps Lock key on by accident while typing.)

> **Change the Color of Text** If you are planning on sending the document over e-mail, you can use colored text. You can also use colored text if you have a color printer. To change the color of the text, select Color from the Style menu and then select a color from the submenu.

Changing the Font Size

In addition to changing the font style, you can change the size of the text. Font sizes are measured in *points*; there are 72 points in an inch. The bigger the size in points, the bigger the font (see Figure 19.3 on the following page).

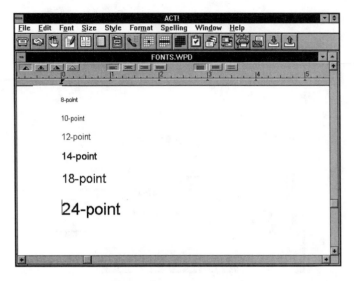

Figure 9.3   Different font sizes.

To change the font size, follow these steps:

1. Select the text you want to format.

2. Open the Size menu to display a list of font sizes.

3. Click on the size you want. ACT! makes the change.

> **Custom Size**   To use a size not listed, select
> Other from the Size menu, and then type the size
> you want and click on OK.

Changing the Font

Using the Style and Size menus, you can change the style and
size—but what if you want to change the font itself? To
change the font, you display the Font dialog box. From this
dialog box, you can select not only the font, but also its style
and size.

To change the font, follow these steps:

1. Open the Font menu and select the Choose command. ACT! displays the Font dialog box (see Figure 19.4 below).

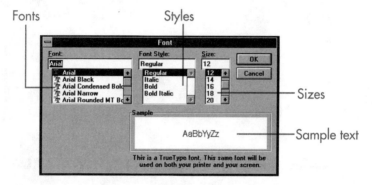

Figure 9.4 The Font dialog box.

2. In the Font list, click on the font you want to use.

3. If you want to change the style also, click on the style you want in the Font Style list.

4. If you want to change the size, click on the size in the Size list.

5. Click on the OK button. ACT! formats the selected text accordingly.

In this lesson you learned about changing the look of text in a document; Lesson 20 explains how to change the format of paragraphs.

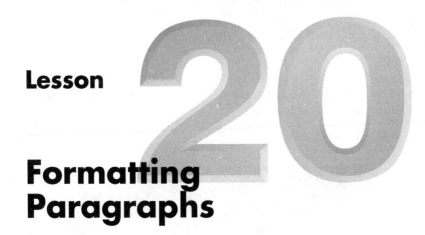

Lesson

Formatting Paragraphs

In this lesson, you learn about some additional ways to change the look of your document: how to change the alignment, indentation, and line spacing for paragraphs.

Aligning Text

All text, by default, aligns with the left margin. This alignment is suitable for most of the body text in a document. For other text (such as headings), you may want to use a different type of alignment—for example, centering your headings. You can also right-align the text, or *full justify* it so that the left and right margins are even. The easiest way to change the alignment is to use the *ruler*.

To change the alignment using the ruler, follow these steps:

1. Select the paragraph you want to align. You can select a single paragraph or several paragraphs.

2. Click on the alignment icon in the ruler (see Figure 20.1 on the following page).

> **Don't See the Ruler?** The ruler should be displayed by default. If it is not, open the Format menu and select the Show Ruler command to display it.

You can also use the Paragraph dialog box to change the alignment. See the section "Using the Paragraph Dialog Box" later in this lesson.

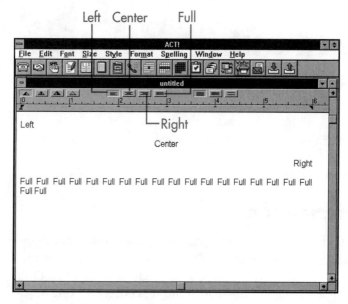

Figure 20.1 Aligning text.

Indenting Text

Another paragraph format you can change is *indents*. Indenting text serves various purposes. Indenting the first line of each paragraph helps the reader easily see where each new paragraph begins. To set off a paragraph-length passage, you may want to indent the entire block from the left margin, or from the left and right margins. For numbered steps, you can use a *hanging indent* (the reverse of a first-line indent). Again, the quickest way to indent text is to use the ruler. You can also use the Paragraph dialog box, as covered later in this lesson.

To indent a paragraph with the ruler, follow these steps:

1. Select the paragraph(s) you want to indent.

2. Drag the indent marker on the ruler to the spot you want (see Figure 20.2). For example, to indent from the left, drag the left indent marker. To indent from the right, drag the right indent marker.

The left-indent marker is really two separate controls that can be dragged separately or together. The triangle is the left-indent marker and controls all lines but the first. The upside-down T-marker controls the indent for the first line.

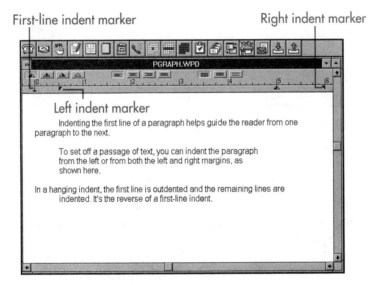

Figure 20.2 Indenting text.

Changing Line Spacing

In addition to changing alignment and indents, you can also use the ruler to change line spacing from the default (single) to double or one-and-a-half spacing. Follow these steps:

1. Select the paragraph(s) you want to change.

2. Click on the spacing icon in the ruler (see Figure 20.3 below).

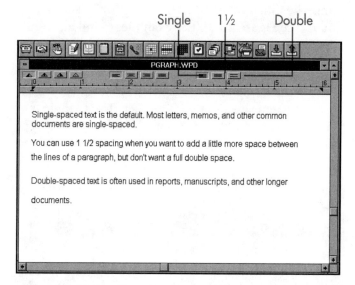

Figure 20.3   Changing line spacing.

Using the Paragraph Dialog Box

In addition to using the ruler, you can use the Paragraph dialog box to format paragraphs. Here you can change many paragraph formats at once (indents, line spacing, and alignment). You also have a little more control over your options when you use the dialog box. For example, you can set line spacing to any interval you want.

To use the Paragraph dialog box to format a paragraph, follow these steps:

1. Select the paragraph(s) you want to change.

2. Open the Format menu and select the Paragraph command. ACT! displays the Paragraph dialog box (see Figure 20.4 on the following page).

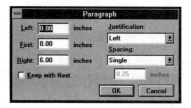

Figure 20.4 The Paragraph dialog box.

3. To change the alignment, display the Justification drop-down list and select the alignment you want.

4. To indent the paragraph(s), do one of the following:

   To indent all lines from the left, enter a value in the Left and First text boxes.

   To indent only the first line from the left, enter a value in the First text box.

   To indent all lines from the right, enter a value in the Right text box.

5. To change the line spacing, display the Spacing drop-down list and select a spacing interval. To set an absolute amount, select Absolute and then enter the amount you want in the text box below.

6. Click on the OK button. ACT! formats the paragraphs with your selections.

Setting Tabs

In your document, you have preset tabs at every inch. If these intervals don't work for your document—or if you want to use one of the other types of tabs (center, left, right, or decimal)—you can change the tabs. The easiest way is to use the ruler. Follow these steps:

1. Select the paragraph(s) for which you want to set new tabs.

2. Click on the type of tab marker you want to set (see Figure 20.5 below).

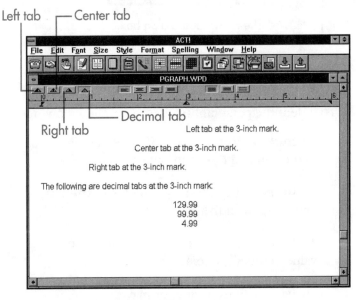

Figure 20.5 Setting tabs.

3. Click on the ruler at the location you have chosen for the tab.

Keep in mind that you can set tabs for each paragraph; when the insertion point is within a paragraph, the ruler displays the tabs (and other paragraph formats) for that paragraph.

Change a Tab To change a tab, simply drag it to a new location on the ruler. To remove a tab, drag it off the ruler.

Lesson

Formatting Pages

In this lesson, you learn how to format pages: insert page breaks, set margins, and create headers and footers.

Inserting Page Breaks

As you type, ACT! adjusts the line breaks within a paragraph as necessary. If you add or delete text, ACT! will move the old text over to make room or to fill in the gaps. ACT! does the same thing for pages. When a page fills up, ACT! inserts a page break and moves to the next page. If you add or delete text, ACT! makes the necessary adjustments.

If you don't like where the page breaks occur, or you want to force a page break, you can insert a page break manually. To do so, open the Format menu and select the Insert Page Break command.

> **Keyboard Shortcut**   Press Shift+Enter to insert a page break.

Setting Margins

When you create a new document, ACT! uses the default margins: one inch at top and bottom, and 1.25 inches at the left and right margins. If these defaults don't work for your documents, you can change them. For instance, to print on letterhead you may need a larger top margin. You can change any of the margins by following these steps:

1. Open the Format menu and select the Page command. ACT! displays the Page Margins dialog box (see Figure 21.1 below).

Figure 21.1   Changing the margins.

2. Click in the text box for the margin you want to change, or press Tab to move to the box.

3. If necessary, delete the current entry. Then type the new value in inches, and click on OK.

Adding Headers and Footers

You may want to include information on each page of a document that identifies the page number and other information (date, document title, your name, and so on). You can include this information in the *header* (text that prints at the top of all pages) or the *footer* (text that prints at the bottom of all pages).

So you can see the page's header and footer areas clearly, start by turning on the page guides. Open the Format menu and select the Show Page Guides command. Then, to create a header or footer, follow these steps:

1. Open the Format menu.

2. To create a header, select the Insert Header command; to create a footer, select the Insert Footer command. ACT! moves you to the top of the document for headers, or to the bottom for footers (see Figure 21.2 on the following page).

3. Type the text you want to include.

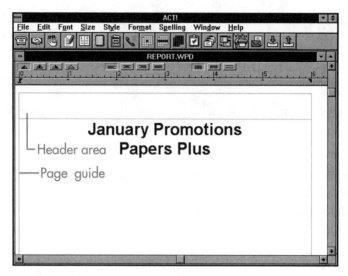

Figure 21.2 Creating a header.

4. To insert any special information you want to include, open the Edit menu and select:

Insert Page Number to have the correct page number automatically inserted.

Insert Date to insert the current date. Select a date format in the dialog box that appears.

Insert Time to insert the current time. Choose whether you want the time updated or not.

5. Click back in the document area when you are finished creating the header or footer.

To modify a header or footer, click in the header or footer area and make any editing or formatting changes you want. To remove a header or footer, open the Format menu and then select the Remove Header (or Remove Footer) command.

Lesson

22

Creating Form Letters

In this lesson, you learn about a special type of document —a letter template or form letter. You can use this type of document when you want to send the same letter to several contacts.

Understanding Templates

In some cases, you may want to send the same letter to several contacts. Perhaps you want to send out a catalog, or a letter announcing new services or products. Rather than create the same letter several times, you can create the letter once, then merge the text of the letter with a single contact, a group of contacts, or all contacts, to create a personalized letter for each contact.

To create these personalized letters, you start with a *template*. A template includes special codes that tell ACT! which information to use from the ACT! contact screen—for example, the name, company name, address, and so on. The template also includes the text of the letter.

You can create a template from scratch and insert the codes and text you want, but it is easier to start with an existing template. ACT! provides several predefined templates that work for different types of documents (letters, envelopes, mailing labels, and so on). These templates include the special codes (which are the most difficult to get right).

You can add the text you want to the template to create a new template. Then, you can merge the text from the template with the contact data, and print the resulting letters. This lesson explains each of these processes.

Editing a Template

As mentioned, ACT! provides several templates you can use to create form letters, order forms, and other document types. You can use one of these templates for a form letter— just add the text. For this lesson, we'll use **letter.tpl**, the same template you use when you create a letter using the Write Letter command.

> **More Templates?** For information on all the templates provided with ACT!, see your ACT! manual.

To edit a template, follow these steps:

1. From a contact screen, open the Write menu and select the Edit Template command. ACT! displays the Select Letter dialog box (see Figure 22.1).

Templates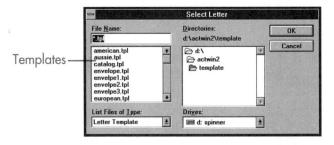

Figure 22.1   Selecting the template to modify.

2. Click on the template you want to change (for example, letter.tpl), and then click on OK. ACT! displays the template on-screen, as in Figure 22.2.

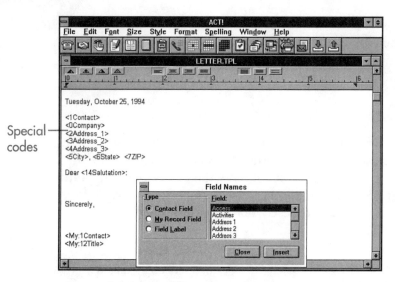

Special codes

Figure 22.2 Modifying a template.

3. Type the text you want to include in the form letter (see Figure 22.3 below).

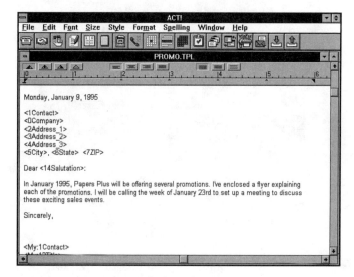

Figure 22.3 A sample form letter.

Close the Dialog Box   If the Field Names dialog box (used for inserting fields) is in your way, you can close it. Click on the Close button.

4. To save the template, open the File menu and select the Save As command. (*Don't* use the Save command; you want to keep the original template intact.)

5. Type a new name for the template and click on the OK button. ACT! saves the template.

Notice the special codes included in the template. These codes tell ACT! to pull information (such as the contact name) from the contact screen. In this template, the letter will include the contact's name, company, address, city, state, ZIP, a salutation, a closing, and your name and title. You don't need to insert any other additional codes— just the text of the document.

The next section explains how to use the template you just created. To close the template, select the File Close command.

Using the Template

The next step in creating a form letter is to merge the template you created with the contacts in your database. You can then review and print the resulting letters. Follow these steps:

1. If you want to send the letter to a single contact, display that contact. To send the letter to a group of contacts, create the lookup group, as covered in Lesson 7.

2. Open the Write menu and select the Form Letter command. ACT! displays the Select Form Letter dialog box (see Figure 22.4 on the following page).

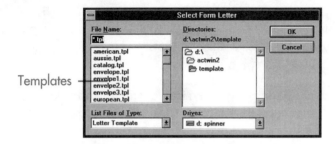

Figure 22.4 Using a template.

3. Select the form letter template; click on the OK button. ACT! displays the Prepare Form Letter dialog box (see Figure 22.5 below).

Figure 22.5 Selecting which contacts to use and where to send the form letters.

4. Select which contacts you want to create form letters for: Active Contact, Active Lookup, or All Contacts.

5. Select where to send the documents: Document, Printer, or E-mail.

6. Click on the OK button.

It's usually a good idea to create a new document in step 5 so you can make sure the letters are what you expected. You can then print the resulting document. Each option in step 5 gives you a different result:

If you select Document, ACT! creates the form letters (see Figure 22.6 below). You can then save or print the document, as described in Lesson 17.

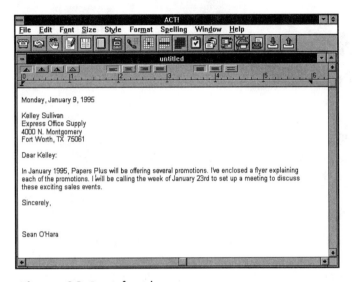

Figure 22.6 A form letter.

If you select Printer, ACT! displays the Print dialog box. Click on the OK button to print the letters.

If you select E-mail, follow the procedures for using your e-mail system to send the letters.

When you print the letters, ACT! will ask whether the documents are finished letters. If they are, click on Yes; ACT! updates the **Letter Date** and **Letter Name** fields for each contact receiving a letter.

In this lesson you learned about a special type of ACT! document—a form letter; Lesson 23 teaches you how to maintain your database and document files.

Lesson 23

Maintaining Your Database

In this lesson, you learn about how to maintain your database and document files—how to back up a database, reindex and compress a database, and delete a document.

Backing Up the Database

Your hard disk is supposed to be a permanent storage device, but unexpected things can happen. The hard disk can crash and you can lose all the information, or you or someone else could accidentally delete some key files.

To protect the information in your database—all the information you toiled to create, update, and keep current—you should make a backup copy of that information periodically. If something goes wrong with the original, you can then use this backup copy and save yourself a lot of work.

ACT! doesn't provide an easy way to back up a database. Instead, you have to make the backups manually. You can use one of the following methods.

Backing Up a Small Database

If your database is relatively small, you may be able to back it up on a single floppy disk. The more records a database contains, the larger its files. A database with just eleven records takes up 138 kilobytes.

If your database is small enough to fit on a floppy disk:

1. Open the File menu and select the Save As command.

2. Insert a blank floppy disk into your diskette drive.

3. In the Save As dialog box, change the Drive designation to that of your floppy drive.

4. Select OK to save the database to the floppy disk.

Backing Up a Large Database

A database is actually several files, all with the same first (or *root*) name, but different extensions. If the database contains many records, all the files for the database might not fit on a single floppy disk.

If that's the case, you must copy the individual files onto as many floppy disks as it takes. For example, to back up the CLIENTS database, you might copy CLIENTS.ADB and CLIENTS.ADX to one disk, and CLIENTS.DBF to another.

> **Where Are They?**   Your database files are stored in the ACTWIN2\DATABASE directory by default.

You can also back up other types of files (such as documents, templates, reports, macros, and so on) by changing to the appropriate directory and copying the files you want to back up.

To copy the individual files, you can use Windows' File Manager, the DOS prompt, or a backup program.

- To use File Manager, first open File Manager. Then open drive windows for your hard disk and for the floppy. Select the database files, and drag them into the drive window for the floppy diskette. For more information about File Manager, see your Windows documentation.

- To use DOS, exit Windows. Change to the directory containing the database files (type **CD\ACTWIN2\ DATABASE**). Then use the **COPY** command to copy the files to the floppy disk. See your DOS documentation for more help.

- To use a backup program (such as MSBACKUP, which comes with DOS versions 6 and above), start the program, choose Backup, and then select the database files as the files you want to back up.

Protecting Your Database

As another way to protect your database, you can assign a password. Without a password, no one else can make changes or display the information in the database. You can assign a password when you create a database initially, or any time after you have created it. In this lesson, I assume you are adding a password to a database you have created previously.

Follow these steps:

1. Open the File menu and select the Database Settings command. ACT! displays the Database Settings dialog box (see Figure 23.1 below).

Figure 23.1 Adding a password.

2. Click on the Password button. ACT! displays the Change Password dialog box (see Figure 23.2 on the following page).

Figure 23.2 Typing a new password.

3. To add a password, press Tab to move to the Enter New Password text box.

4. Type the password and click on the OK button. ACT! prompts you to confirm the password.

5. Type the password again and click OK. ACT! assigns the password to the database; the Change Password dialog box closes.

6. Click on the OK button to close the Database Settings dialog box.

Once you have added a password and then try to open the database, ACT! will prompt you for the password. Type the password and click on the OK button.

> **Don't Forget Your Password** If your company's security policy allows it (check first!), you might want to write down your password and keep the note somewhere safe. If you forget your password, you won't be able to access the database.

Purging, Reindexing, and Compressing Your Database

If you find that your database is getting too big and ACT! is not working as quickly as it used to, you may want to consider *purging* (deleting) some information. Specifically, you can purge contact notes and histories to free up disk space and speed performance. You can purge the notes and/or histories for all contacts or a group of contacts; you can also select a date range to purge.

As part of maintenance, you can reindex and compress the database. Do this especially after you have deleted several records. Reindexing helps ACT! find records more quickly, and compressing regains the disk space that was used by the deleted contacts.

You can use the Maintenance command to purge, reindex, and compress your database. Follow these steps:

1. Open the File menu and select the Maintenance command. ACT! displays the Maintenance dialog box (see Figure 23.3 below).

Figure 23.3 Purging, reindexing, or compressing your database.

2. To purge the database, check the items you want to purge: Purge Notes and/or Purge History.

3. To compress and reindex, select the Compress and reindex database option. Use this option if you have deleted a substantial number of contacts. If you have not deleted contacts and just want to reindex, select the Reindex database option.

4. Click on the OK button.

If you just reindexed and compressed, ACT! carries out the procedure. Skip the remaining steps.

If you selected to purge notes and histories, you see an on-screen calendar. Follow the remaining steps.

5. Drag across the range you want to purge. If you want to purge all dates, click on the All Dates button. To purge all past dates, click on the Past button.

ACT! purges the notes or histories from the database. You see a status bar that displays the progress of the purge. If you also reindexed and compressed, you see a status bar of this procedure as well.

Deleting a Document

The final maintenance feature you may want to use is the Delete command. You can use this command to delete documents you no longer need. Doing so frees up disk space for other files. You can delete any type of document—databases, templates, reports, word processing documents, and so on.

Be Careful Be sure you really don't need the file before you delete it. You cannot undo the deletion without a special Undelete utility. (DOS 5 and 6 include an Undelete command, as do other popular utility programs such as Norton Utilities.)

Follow these steps to delete a document:

1. Open the File menu and select the Delete command. You see the Delete File dialog box (as shown in Figure 23.4 on the following page).

Delete What? The Delete File dialog box lists daabase files if you started from the contact screen, or word processing documents if you started from the word processing screen. You can change the type of file that is displayed by following step 2 of the deletion procedure.

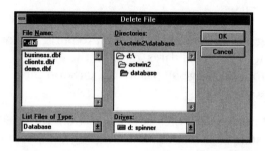

Figure 23.4 Deleting a file.

2. If necessary, display the List Files of Type drop-down list; select the type of file you want to delete.

3. In the File Name list, select the file you want to delete.

4. Click on the OK button. ACT! prompts you to confirm the deletion.

5. Click on the Yes button to delete the file. (Click on the No button if you've changed your mind.) ACT! deletes the file.

In this lesson you learned about some of the important maintenance features you can use to keep ACT! and your computer performing at optimum level; Lesson 24 explains some ways you can customize ACT!

Lesson

Customizing ACT!

You can customize some features of ACT! so that the program works just the way you want. This lesson covers some of the changes you may want to consider making, including setting program preferences and creating macros.

Customizing Program Preferences

ACT! enables you to change many of the defaults used in the program—from where the icon bar and status bars are displayed to how the speller works. Table 24.1 explains the different sets of preferences you can change.

Table 24.1 ACT! preferences.

Preference	Use to
Alarm Settings	Set the default lead time and duration for calls, meetings, and to-dos. You can also use it to control whether ACT! performs automatic checks for schedule conflicts and sets alarms.
Bar Position	Control where the icon bar is placed (top, left, right, or bottom) and where the status bar appears (top, left, right, or bottom).

continues

Table 24.1 Continued

Preference	Use to
Custom Icons	Delete existing icons or add new icons to the icon bar.
Dialing Settings	Enter the modem setup initialization string, as well as the settings for port and phone type. You can also use it to enter any prefixes or postfixes for phone numbers.
E-mail	Enter any initial text for messages, select a display font, and control in what order messages are displayed in the inbox.
Miscellaneous	Set miscellaneous options such as which key moves you from field to field (Tab or Enter), whether the database is saved automatically, whether the spell check displays alternative spellings by default, and whether a WinFAX icon is included in the icon bar.
Name Separators	Add first-name prefixes, last-name prefixes, or last-name suffixes so that ACT! knows how to separate the names in the Contact field.
Path Defaults	Set the default directory for different file types.
Schedule Icon Defaults	Control whether the Call, Meeting, and To-do buttons are used to schedule a new activity or modify an existing activity.

Preference	Use to
Schedule Settings	Set which popups appear for date, time, duration, and lead time. This setting also controls popups regarding fields for calls, meetings, and to-dos. You can also use it to roll over certain activities automatically.
Startup Settings	Select a macro to run or a file to open on startup.

To make a change to any of these preferences, follow these steps:

1. Open the Edit menu and select the Preferences command. ACT! displays the Preferences dialog box (see Figure 24.1 below).

Figure 24.1 Setting ACT! preferences.

2. In the Modify list, select the setting you want to change. The options in the right side of the dialog box will vary on the basis of the selected option.

3. Make any changes.

4. Click on the OK button.

Creating Macros

A *macro* is a powerful feature that you can use to futher customize ACT! Macros automate routine tasks such as sorting by last name, making text bold, switching to a layout group, and so on. If you find yourself performing the same set of commands over and over, you can create a macro to execute all the commands automatically in their correct sequence.

Macro   A series of steps you record so you can play them back later automatically.

Try Some of ACT!'s Macros   ACT! includes several useful macros that enable you to quickly perform common tasks, such as, making text bold, underlining text, printing an address book, closing a database, and several others.

This section explains how to create or record a macro, and then how to run (play back) that macro.

Recording a Macro

The first step in creating a macro is to plan what you want the macro to do. What is its purpose? What commands do you want the macro to include?

After you know what you want to do, creating a macro is pretty simple. You turn on the recorder, perform the steps you want to record, and then turn off the recorder. ACT! notes everything you do, from the time the recorder is turned on until it is turned off.

Follow these steps to record a macro:

1. Open the Edit menu, select the Macro command, and select the Record Macro command from the submenu that appears. ACT! displays the Record Macro dialog box (see Figure 24.2 below).

Keyboard Shortcut Press Alt+F5 to start the macro recorder.

Record Macro	
Name:	
Description:	
Mouse:	Record Clicks and Drags
	Record Cancel

Figure 24.2 Naming the macro.

2. In the Name text box, type a name of up to eight characters.

Name That Macro When you name your macro, ACT! assigns it the extension **.MAC** and stores the macro file in the C:\ACTWIN2 \MAC-ROS directory.

3. If you want, type a description in the Description text box.

4. To specify what actions are recorded, display the Mouse drop-down list and select which options to record. Select Clicks and Drags to record only mouse actions. Select Everything to record both keyboard actions and mouse actions. Select Ignore Mouse to record only keyboard actions.

5. Click on the Record button.

Be Careful! Everything you select—every command, mouse action, and key press—is recorded until you stop the recorder.

6. Perform the actions you want to record.

7. To stop the recorder, open the Edit menu, select the Macro command, and then the Stop Macro command.

Playing Back a Macro

Once you have recorded the macro, you can play it back at any time by following these steps:

Start at the Right Spot Before you play back your macro, make sure the record or document you want to work with is displayed on-screen; ACT! will carry out the macro's commands on whatever is in the current window.

1. Open the Edit menu, select the Macro command, and select the Run Macro command. ACT! displays the Run Macro dialog box (see Figure 24.3 below).

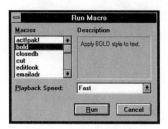

Figure 24.3 Playing back a macro.

2. In the Macros list, select the macro you want to run.

3. Click on the Run button. ACT! plays back the macro.

> **Macro Doesn't Work**   If the macro doesn't
> work the way you wanted, you can re-record it.
> Follow the steps in the section "Creating a
> Macro;" then type the same name you used when
> you initially created the macro. ACT! will ask whether
> you want to replace the existing macro. Click on the Yes
> button. Then re-record the steps.

If you don't need a macro anymore—or created a macro that was so haywire you want to get rid of it—you can delete it. Open the Edit menu, select the Macro command, and select Delete Macro from the submenu. Select the macro you want to delete, and then click on the Delete button. Click on the Yes button to confirm the deletion.

This lesson completes the *Ten Minute Guide to ACT!*. I hope you enjoyed it. You should now be able to put ACT!'s features and commands to work for you.

Index

T

tabs, setting, 135-136
Task List command
    (View menu), 92
task lists, 92-95
    displaying, 92
    modifying, 94-97
    priority lookups, 94
    viewing range of dates, 93
templates, 140-145
text
    adding, 109
    aligning, 131-132
    colors, 128
    copying, 111
    deleting, 109
    finding, 112-113
    fonts, changing, 127-130
    indents, changing, 132-133
    inserting, 105-106
    line spacing, changing, 133-134
    moving, 110-111
    replacing, 113-115
    selecting, 107-108
    spelling, checking, 115-116
    tabs, setting, 135-136
Timeless button, 74
Timer dialog box, 78
timing calls, 78-79
To-do command
    (Schedule menu), 83
To-do field, 84
Totals command (View menu), 96

U-V

Undo command (Edit menu), 109
View Group dialog box, 62
View Task List button, 92
viewing
    calendars, 86-88
    contact lists, 66-67
    contacts, 65-67

notes, 24
task lists, 92

W-Z

wildcards, (*), 55
Windows, starting, 1
windows
    ACT!, 2-8
    note, 23-24
word processor
    aligning, 131-132
    documents
        closing, 119
        creating, 104-105
        navigating, 106-107
        opening, 119-120
        printing, 120
        saving, 117-118
    faxes, 124-125
    indents, changing, 132-133
    letters, creating, 121
    line spacing, changing, 133-134
    margins, setting, 137-138
    memos, creating, 123-124
    page breaks, inserting, 137
    tabs, setting, 135-136
    templates, 141-143
    text
        adding, 109
        colors, 128
        copying, 111
        deleting, 109
        finding, 112-113
        fonts, 127-130
        moving, 110-111
        replacing, 113-115
        selecting, 107-108
        typing, 105-106
    word wraps, 105

Yes button, 12